D1450094

PHOTOSHOP® AND DREAMWEAVER® INTEGRATION:

CREATING HIGH-IMPACT WEB PAGES

COLIN SMITH

McGraw-Hill/Osborne

New York Chicago San Francisco
Lisbon London Madrid Mexico City
Milan New Delhi San Juan
Seoul Singapore Sydney Toronto

The **McGraw·Hill** Companies

McGraw-Hill/Osborne
2100 Powell Street, 10th Floor
Emeryville, California 94608
U.S.A.

To arrange bulk purchase discounts for sales promotions, premiums, or fund-raisers, please contact **McGraw-Hill**/Osborne at the above address. For information on translations or book distributors outside the U.S.A., please see the International Contact Information page immediately following the index of this book.

Photoshop® and Dreamweaver® Integration: Creating High-Impact Web Pages

1234567890 VNH VNH 0198765
ISBN 0-07-225588-9

Vice President & Group Publisher PHILIP RUPPEL	**Copy Editor** LISA THEOBALD
Vice President & Publisher JEFFREY KRAMES	**Proofreader** SUSIE ELKIND
Acquisitions Editor MARJORIE MCANENY	**Indexer** CLAIRE SPLAN
Executive Project Editor MARK KARMENDY	**Creative Director** SCOTT JACKSON
Acquisitions Coordinator AGATHA KIM	**Graphic Designer** D. MICHAEL PITALO
Technical Editor JEFF KEYSER	**Cover Design** COLIN SMITH

This book was composed with QuarkXPress.

Information has been obtained by **McGraw-Hill**/Osborne from sources believed to be reliable. However, because of the possibility of human or mechanical error by our sources, **McGraw-Hill**/Osborne, or others, **McGraw-Hill**/Osborne does not guarantee the accuracy, adequacy, or completeness of any information and is not responsible for any errors or omissions or the results obtained from the use of such information.

For Jim Clark. Who was more than an Uncle.

ABOUT THE AUTHOR

Colin Smith is a best-selling author, trainer, and award-winning new-media designer who has caused a stir in the design community with his stunning photorealistic illustrations composed entirely in Photoshop. He is founder of the world's most popular Photoshop resource site, PhotoshopCAFE.com, which boasts more than two million visitors.

With over ten years of experience in the design industry, Colin was formerly Senior Editor and Art Director for *VOICE* magazine. He is a regular columnist for *Photoshop User* magazine, PlanetPhotoshop.com, as well as for the official site of the National Association for Photoshop Professionals. He also contributes to a number of other graphic art publications, such as *Mac Design* magazine, *Web Designer* magazine and *Computer Arts* magazine.

Colin's graphic design work has been recognized with numerous awards, including the Guru awards at Photoshop World 2001 and 2002, for his work in both illustration and web design. He's authored or co-authored more than ten books on Photoshop, including the best-selling *How to Do Everything with Photoshop CS* (McGraw-Hill/Osborne, 2003) and award-winning *Photoshop Most Wanted: Effects and Design Tips* (A Press/Friends of Ed, 2002). Colin is also creator of the *Photoshop Secrets* video training series (PhotoshopCD.com). He is in high demand across the United States as a lecturer, presenting his Photoshop techniques to Web designers and other graphics professionals across the nation.

ABOUT THE TECHNICAL EDITOR

Jeff Keyser is an award-winning art director, designer, and developer who has produced projects for a variety of high-profile clients including Nike, ESPN, Billabong, Adidas, Universal, and a host of others. This experience has allowed him to work with a wide group of ad agencies and design houses across the country, spanning the mediums of interactive, broadcast, print, and DVD.

Jeff's work has been honored with numerous awards in shows including The One Show, Cannes International Advertising Festival, and multiple Flash Film Festivals throughout the US and Europe.

His work can be seen at **jeffkeyser.com**.

CONTENTS

Acknowledgments xiii

Introduction xv

PART I — PREPARE TO BUILD THE SITE

CHAPTER 1

Plan and Wireframe Your New Site

Plan and Wireframe Your New Site 1

A Brief History of the Internet 2

History of Web Design Editors 3

Files on the Internet 4

Building a Web Site: Wireframing 5

　　Discovery Phase 6

　　Content Organization Phase 6

　　Creative Discovery Phase 8

　　Comp Creation 11

　　Pull It All Together 11

CHAPTER 2

Understand and Use Color and Imagery to Reinforce the Message

Understand and Use Color and Imagery to Reinforce the Message . . . 13

Talking with Color 14

　　Color Anatomy 14

　　Choosing Colors 15

　　Using Photoshop's Color Palette and Color Picker to Create Colors 16

　　Building a Color Palette 19

　　Swatches Palette 20

Understanding Color Combinations 22

　　The Color Wheel 23

Choosing a Texture 25

　　Tiling Backgrounds 26

Choosing Images 32

CHAPTER 3

Design the Interface and Navigation **35**

Creating a New Document 36
Creating the Layout in Photoshop. 37
Creating the Navigation 40
    Creating a Glassy Button 42
    Adding the Buttons to the Main Page 47
    Duplicating and Aligning Elements on a Page. 48
Adding "Eye Candy" to the Page 50
    Creating the Illusion of Depth 52
Adding a Secondary Rollover Interface. 56

PART II — PREPARE THE FILES FOR THE WEB

CHAPTER 4

Create Image Maps and Rollovers with Slices **61**

Slicing Basics 62
    The Zone System 62
    What Is Slicing?. 63
    Slicing Strategies 65
Slicing Your Project 70
Using Tables to Organize Slices. 73
    Converting Slices to Tables. 74
    Manual Slicing 76
    Slicing the Navigation—Creating Layer-Based Slices. 78
    Renaming Slices 83
Creating Image Maps 83
Creating a Rollover Effect 85
    Remote Rollovers. 89
    Adding Hyperlinks to the Buttons 90

CHAPTER 5

The Need for Speed: Making the Page Load Quickly and Efficiently . . 93

Why Optimize? 94

Measuring Image Size and Speed 94

    The Easy Way to Calculate Download Times 95

Viewing Optimized Images 95

Choosing the Correct Way to Compress Your Images. 96

    GIF (Graphics Interchange Format) 97

    JPEG (Joint Photographic Experts Group) 101

    PNG (Portable Network Graphics). 103

    SWF (Macromedia Flash). 104

Optimizing Sliced Images 104

    Selecting Multiple Slices 104

    Fine-Tuning the Optimization Settings. 107

Adding Hyperlinks 110

Adding E-mail Links 112

Exporting. 113

Save for Web 115

PART III — WORK IN DREAMWEAVER

CHAPTER 6

Building the Home Page. 117

Setting Up a New Site in Dreamweaver 118

Opening a Page in Dreamweaver 122

Using the Dreamweaver Workspace. 124

    Maximizing Your Screen Area. 127

    Finding Help. 128

    Ordering the Tables 129

Preparing the Content Zone of Your Design 131

    Creating a Nested Table 134

Creating Custom Content Boxes in Photoshop/Dreamweaver 139

    Exporting Select Slices from ImageReady. 141

    Centering the Table 145

    Setting an Image as a Repeating Background 146

CHAPTER 7

Streamlining the Process—Using Cascading Style Sheets and Templates **155**

Cascading Style Sheets 156
   How CSS Works 157
   Advantages of CSS... 158
   Creating Your First CSS Style................................. 158
Templates... 169
   Converting a Page to a Template 170
   Using Templates.. 174
Creating Hyperlinks 177
   Creating Text Hyperlinks 177
   Changing the Appearance of a Hyperlink 179

CHAPTER 8

Creating the Whole Site **185**

The Site Map... 186
   Viewing the Site Map 186
Creating New Pages.. 189
   Method 1: Creating Pages from the Files Panel 189
   Method 2: Applying a Template to an Existing Page 191
   Method 3: Renaming Existing Pages 196
   Finishing Up 197
Placing Images in Dreamweaver 198
Importing Text into Dreamweaver................................ 200
   Changing Line Spacing 201

CHAPTER 9

Add Movement and Interactivity **205**

Transparency 206
   Preparing the Image 206
   Optimizing and Matting 207
   Animations 209

Creating a Sliding Animation 209
   Creating a Fading Animation and Inserting It with Dreamweaver 215
   Adding the Animation to Your Web Page 217
Creating Rollovers in Dreamweaver 218
   Preparing the Rollover Graphics in Photoshop 219
   Adding a Rollover Image to Dreamweaver 221
Behaviors 223
   Creating a Rollover Using Behaviors 224
   Removing a Behavior 225
Creating Drop-down (Pop-up) Menus 226
   Making Multitiered Menus 228

PART IV — MOVE BEYOND YOUR LOCAL COMPUTER

CHAPTER 10

Create Forms and E-Commerce Capabilities 231

Forms 232
   Creating a Form 233
   Creating Buttons 238
   Creating a Checkbox 239
   Making the Form Work 241
Create a Jump Menu 243
E-Commerce 245
   Signing Up for a PayPal Account 246
   Creating a Buy Now Button 248

CHAPTER 11

Adding the Cool Factor 257

Using Frames to Create an Image Gallery 258
   Setting Frame Properties 261
   Creating Pages to Load into the Frame 262
   Considerations in Using Frames 265
Creating a Picture Gallery Using Photoshop's Automation Tools 265
   Setting the Options 268
Creating Inline Frames (Iframes) 271
   Loading New Pages into the Iframe 274

Creating Pop-up Windows 277
    Closing a Window 280
    Creating a Close Button 281
Jump Menus 282
Building a Liquid Site 284

CHAPTER 12

Going Live: Uploading Your Site to the Web 291

Obtaining a Hosting Account 292
Registering a Domain Name 295
Linking Your Domain Name with Your Hosting Account 298
Uploading Your Pages to the Web Server 300
    Connecting Dreamweaver to the Web Server 300
    Uploading the Site to the Web Server 302
Maintaining and Managing Your Site 304
    Synchronization 304
    Checking for Broken Links 306
Conclusion 308

Index 309

ACKNOWLEDGMENTS

There are a few people I would like to thank. Without their hard work, patience, and insight, this book never would have happened.

To the OMG team: Katie Conley for going to bat on this project. Margie McAneny for picking up the baton and running to the finish line. Agatha Kim for keeping everything flowing in a pleasant way. Mark Karmendy for keeping it all on track. Lisa Theobald, thanks for making me sound literate; and thanks, Scott Jackson, for making it all look good and being enthusiastic through all our design changes. Thanks to Kate for your great marketing efforts.

Thanks to my buddy Jeff Keyser for your awesome job of tech editing.

Thanks to Gwyn Weisberg from Adobe Systems; we will make it sushi next time, I promise. Thanks to Heather Hollaender from Macromedia for your support and help on this and other projects. My buddy in the business, Al Ward (I'll send you the phone bill). Scott and Jeff Kelby, Chris Main, Dave Cross, Stacy Behan, Felix Nelson, and everyone else from KW that I haven't mentioned. Thanks to the Deidrich crew, especially Ali Sabet, Michael Donnellan, and Allen Obciana.

Thanks to everyone at the CAFÉ. Especially all the awesome Mods and Admins who keep things going smoothly and in the right spirit. You are the best! To all my online buddies, Phunk, Nina, Mark Monciardini, Malachi, Jay, Trevor Morris, Ryan, Jens Karlsson, and many others I have neglected to mention, thanks for the synergy and making things more fun!

Thanks to my friends, Mauriahh, Vlad, Mel, Jason (officer) King, Nancy, Mark, and Tiff, Tom Leding, Rob Deluca, Andy, George and Hazel, Joel, Tim Cooper, Steve and Tanis, and others. Thanks go out to my parents, especially my Mum. I have always felt lucky to have such an awesome mother. My sister Carolyn and Samuel. Audrey, Isabel, Roy and Bev, Phillip and Irene, thanks. Thanks to God for giving me the gifts I have and allowing me to use them in the way I enjoy.

INTRODUCTION

Ask a professional Web designer what the preferred tools of the trade are and you will hear the same thing again and again: Adobe Photoshop and Macromedia Dreamweaver. These are the leading programs used to create HTML-based Web sites. Adobe Photoshop, the leading image editing and creation application, has enjoyed the unrivaled position at the top of the design industry for years. Photoshop also comes bundled with a secret weapon called ImageReady. ImageReady is bursting with features that make creating images for the Web a snap. Macromedia Dreamweaver is the favored tool for taking all these beautiful graphics and arranging them for display on the Web. Of course, Dreamweaver's feature set goes way beyond merely displaying images. It brings complex technologies down to the grass-roots level for ordinary people to use—CSS, JavaScript behaviors, tables, frames, DHTML, and even server technology are within reach of the mere mortal, thanks to this robust application.

The question arises, with all these powerful tools at our disposal, where do we start? How can we figure out a workflow that will enable us to navigate this combined endless array of features, finding just the ones needed to get the job done? Not just that, but we want our pages to look like those of the pros. This book is written as a response to this need. In the pages of this book you will learn a real-world workflow that incorporates Photoshop and Dreamweaver. You will learn how to take an idea from a scribble on a sheet of paper to a fully functional Web site that boasts powerful interactivity and ecommerce. Everything you need to make this happen is between the covers of this book. Best of all, you don't have to be a rocket scientist to do it—invest a weekend with this book and your Web pages will never be the same!

We will begin by exploring some basic design principles. You will learn how to use color and images for maximum impact. We will discuss different types of design and even how to work with clients. At the end of the first section you will know how to plan a site and create a wire frame.

Next, we will create some stunning graphics using Photoshop. You will learn some of the tricks of the trade and little secrets like creating inset lines and realistic-looking buttons.

We'll then take the design into ImageReady and optimize the images for lightning-fast download times. You will learn all about slicing and rollovers. We will add a few little tricks in ImageReady and then export the page to HTML.

After we have pushed Photoshop and ImageReady to the max, we will pass the baton to Dreamweaver. We will do a quick orientation for users who are new to Dreamweaver and then crank things up. You will learn how to arrange your pages into tables and we will look at a few graphics tricks such as creating cool-looking boxes to hold our content. We will explore style sheets and templates so that you can quickly turn a single page into an entire site.

As we progress, such cool features as iframes, liquid sites, drop-down menus, forms, and jump menus will be demystified. We will even explore how you can get ecommerce on your site today without spending any money!

Finally (where most books end), we will walk through the process of signing up for a Web hosting account, registering a domain name, and hooking it all up together. We will wrap up the book by uploading your site to the Web and a learning a few important site-maintenance tips.

As you can see, this book will not just show you how to design a page and then leave you hanging. You'll actually learn how to upload your site for the world to see.

Congratulations on picking up this book. Perhaps you are currently using Photoshop and have no idea how to leverage your existing skills to create a Web site. Alternatively, you may already be proficient with Photoshop and Dreamweaver and just need to find out the best way to use these technologies together. Whatever your experience level, this book will show you how to do the things you have always wanted to do in a way that you will understand. This book is not written by a scientist or technician—it's written by someone who works in the design field every day. The methods shown here are proven to work in the real world, not just the classroom.

I have written this book in a way that you can either follow along from beginning to end or jump directly to the topic that most interests you. If you are new to Web design, I highly recommend that you begin at the front and work your way through the entire book, as there are many lessons and tips to be learned from these pages. Although the book is written in such a way that you can follow along with the shown example, I would recommend that you explore your creativity and create your own design. The chapters are written in such a way that the techniques can be adapted for almost any type of design.

> ### NOTE
>
> I have assumed that the reader will have at least a basic understanding of Photoshop. If not, I recommend my book, *How to Do Everything with Photoshop CS* (McGraw-Hill/Osborne). But even if you are brand-new to Dreamweaver or have never created a Web site, this is the book for you.

I hope you enjoy using this book as much as I have enjoyed writing it.

PART I

PREPARE TO BUILD THE SITE

CHAPTER 1

PLAN AND WIREFRAME YOUR NEW SITE

A lot has happened in the few years since the World Wide Web was introduced to the public; since then, it has become a household word. We have seen a veritable "gold rush" to get a piece of the online market and the dot-com crash; now, perhaps more stable times are ahead. Today, an online presence is no longer a luxury; it's a business necessity. Businesses need to be visible on the Web, whether simply for PR purposes or because a virtual storefront is required to sell a product. People use the Web daily to perform research, shop for tickets and other goods, check schedules, pay bills, or just be entertained.

The tools used to create web sites are almost as numerous as the reasons for using it. As technology progresses at breakneck speeds, web designers struggle to keep up. Two tools have emerged as champions at the top of the heap of options and are recognized as the industry standards: Adobe Photoshop and Macromedia Dreamweaver are the world's most popular software combination to use for building visually appealing professional web sites.

Photoshop is, without question, the world's most popular image-editing application. Bundled with Photoshop is a not-so-secret weapon called ImageReady, which helps you prepare graphics for use on the Web. ImageReady was released around the time of Photoshop 5's release with one purpose: to build web graphics. Version 5.5 of Photoshop saw ImageReady integrated, or rather "bundled," because it would launch as a separate program. Photoshop/ImageReady CS marks the first version with true integration, as they both now share the same image window. This version is packed with lots of goodies to make web designers' lives much easier. Throughout the course of this book, we will use many of these features.

A BRIEF HISTORY OF THE INTERNET

The Internet was invented by a group of scientists who were looking for a more efficient way of sharing code and formulas across long distances. The idea was to connect multiple computers over telephone lines and networks to transfer information to and from each other. HTML (HyperText Markup Language) was invented as the language for this purpose. Using HTML, you can assign hyperlinks to any piece of text. With a click of the link, the user is transported to another place within the document or to an entirely different document. This is a very efficient way to organize large chunks of information (and it sure beats the old microfiche system). Basic HTML is a very simple code to learn, and anyone can write it without too much effort. To convert HTML to something that is readable to humans, we use a web browser. Currently the most popular web browsers are Microsoft Internet Explorer, Netscape Navigator, and Apple Safari. These browsers decode the HTML and display it in a user-friendly, visual way.

The Internet came of age in the early 1990s and began its mainstream life. In 1994, the World Wide Web Consortium (W3C) was formed to set standards for HTML and other web technologies. During this time, the Internet culture was young and all about sharing information, and an unwritten honor system existed. The spirit of the Web was "take a little and give a little." Quality information began to stream down the lines as eager pioneers shared their knowledge and time with others who were willing to help lay the Internet's foundations. It was this spirit of sharing that inspired me to begin PhotoshopCAFE.com, a community that gives back to the Web by providing free resources and tutorials. Unfortunately, in some ways the Web lost its innocence when its commercial appeal was realized and has since been plagued with spam—unsolicited junk mail—spyware, and viruses. The information superhighway has become somewhat of an information supermarket.

The Internet quickly developed from its humble beginnings, and other technologies emerged, such as the ability to upload images and sound clips. Things quickly snowballed as other programming languages such as Java and JavaScript made interactive features a reality. Macromedia released Shockwave and acquired a small program called Future Splash, which developed into the blockbuster we now know as Flash. Databases were connected to web pages and the web pages grew up into full-blown web applications. The Internet is still very much in its infancy, and the future is bright; it's up to us to determine exactly how that future unfolds.

HISTORY OF WEB DESIGN EDITORS

Back in the early 1990s, the only way to build a web page was to use applications like Notepad or Simple Text and write the HTML code yourself. Programs such as HoTMetaL emerged, which helped with the coding, but WYSIWYG (what you see is what you get) web page editors were merely a figment of the imagination. Software giant Microsoft was accused of all but ignoring the Internet. I must confess that at the time I thought that the Web was just a passing fad. Very quickly, though, I (and many others) realized that the Web was here to stay.

Microsoft kicked off the WYSIWYG race with a little web scripting program called FrontPage. At the time, nothing like it was available on the market, and if you could stand your HTML code being mutilated and all kinds of proprietary "web-bots,"

FrontPage was an alternative to hand-coding. Soon, however, Macromedia announced the release of Dreamweaver. Everyone was excited about this program because of a feature called "round-trip HTML" editing, which let you open your code in Dreamweaver, switch to WYSIWYG view, add some elements, and then go back to code view—and all the HTML would remain intact. Today, FrontPage, as well as other programs such as Adobe's own GoLive, support round-trip HTML. Still, Dreamweaver has established itself as the clear winner in the web-design race to date. Naturally, many features have been added over time, including integration of UltraDev, a WYSIWYG back-end code editor that connects databases.

> **NOTE**
>
> In this book, we concentrate on front-end web design. Back-end programmer/ developer stuff is beyond the scope of this book (and the interest of many designers).

FILES ON THE INTERNET

After a user creates a web page, it is uploaded to a *web server*, a computer that is permanently connected to the Internet and is available for other computers to connect to and access the information that resides on it (such as your web page). A web surfer can access this information in a web browser by entering a unique address, known as a Domain Name (such as http://www.dreamweavercafe.com). The *http://* part says it's a hypertext document that has been coded with HTML. The *www* is World Wide Web, and *.com* is the extension for a company. Here are some of the many file extensions you'll see in Domain names:

EXTENSION	MEANING		EXTENSION	MEANING
.com	Company		.biz	Business
.edu	Educational institution		.uk	Britain
.org	Organization		.nz	New Zealand
.net	Internet service		.au	Australia
.gov	US government		.de	Germany

When you create your web page and save the files to your hard disk, the page is called a *local site*. The files will all be stored in a local directory. These files will consist of such things as HTML documents, images, sound files, and video clips. An HTML page is not capable of displaying images on its own; instead, it references images stored with the file and then displays them in the page.

Before the world can see the web page, it has to be moved to a server. This is called a *remote connection* because the files are stored in a different location (that is, not on your computer's hard drive). (We will get into the mechanics of this when the need arises later on in the book.)

BUILDING A WEB SITE: WIREFRAMING

Many of my potential clients ask a question I always find amusing: "How much does a web site cost?" I usually respond with, "How long is a piece of string?" I mean, it all depends on what is required.

Before we begin the process of building a web page, we need to do some planning. This planning stage is called *wireframing*. The *wireframe* is a plan that brings information together. It includes the main features of a site and a site map, and perhaps a rough sketch of the design—at the least sketching out where the features will fit on the site.

Discovery Phase

The first step of wireframing is the discovery phase. Following are some of the mechanical facts you will need to discover:

- How much content is required?
- What industry will this serve?
- How many images will be provided?
- How many images will have to be created?
- Will content be written?
- How complex is the navigation?
- Will interactive features be included?
- What other technologies will be used?
- Will ongoing maintenance be required?

Once you have discovered the hard facts, you may be in a position to provide an estimated cost to a client, but you will not yet be ready to begin the creative side of the process.

Content Organization Phase

Content should be organized into categories. Think of the web site as a house; in web terms, here's what the house analogy means:

- The *house* is the entire web site. (The *neighborhood* may be links to other, external sites.)
- The *rooms* are the top-level pages or main links on a home page. Room names will appear on the navigation bar. I recommend that you include

no more that seven top-level pages; any more than that, and the navigation becomes cluttered and confusing.

- The *closets* are the sub-pages or sub-links, pages that are linked to and accessed from the top-level pages. For example, a top-level category may be titled "Gallery." The gallery contains links to each category of images such as sketches, photographs and paintings. These categories are the sub-links on a page.

Try to consolidate wherever possible. For instance, a map to the client's physical location could be added to the "About Us" page. Once the content is organized into categories, try to provide meaningful names for each section. Keep these names short—single words, if possible. Following are some common top-level names:

HOME	ABOUT US	VISION	MISSION	LINKS	GALLERY	CONTACT
ORDER	STORE	PRESS	ACCOLADES	SERVICES	EVENTS	STAFF

The list of possibilities is really endless, but these should help provide a springboard.

Once you have decided how the content will be organized, sketch it out on a piece of paper as a basic site map. This map is a flow chart that outlines the hierarchical organization of the web site. It is worth the investment of time to plan at this stage. We have not even considered the visuals yet. It would be like an architect trying to draw up plans without even considering how many bedrooms or bathrooms will be in the house. It's been said, "If you fail to plan, you plan to fail." The initial site map can be nicely formatted and color-coded or as simple as a few words jotted on a napkin. Figure 1-1 shows a basic site map of DreamweaverCAFE.com; something similar to this is sufficient for most designers to work from as a guide of the structure. (See the end of this chapter for the site planning sheet that I use for my company.)

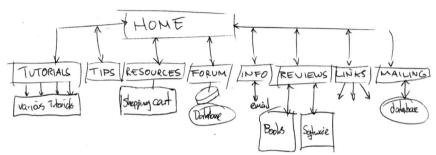

Figure 1–1: A basic site map

Creative Discovery Phase

At this time, we can begin to think about basic look and feel. You should meet for
another interview with the client—for this meeting, I suggest you do a bit of steer-
ing. You should have conducted some research by now—looked at the industry
and noticed how the competitors' sites are arranged. At this meeting, you need to
find out more about the creative side of things. Some of the information you will
need includes the following:

- What kind of "style" will best serve the client's needs? For example,
  a high-tech style will not work for an antique store; nor will a high-
  energy bright design work for a funeral home.

- What competitor sites does the client like, and why do they like them?
  What don't they like?

- What kind of budget will you be working with? (You cannot always get
  the answer to this because some clients will hesitate, hoping that you
  have a smaller initial figure in mind than they do, or they may just have
  no idea.)

- What colors do they love or hate? Although it's a good idea to use colors that best convey the "feel" you are trying to achieve (as discussed

in Chapter 2), your efforts will be a waste of time if the client hates those colors.

- Any graphic elements that must or must not appear on the site? (You would be surprised.)
- Does the company have a logo yet, and can it be provided as an EPS (Encapsulated PostScript) or Illustrator file?

> **TIP**
>
> Although in a perfect world all the best decisions will make good design sense, we are living in a world in which clients may have their own ideas. Good or bad, remember the client is paying the bill and he/she is your boss.

Once you have done some discovery, it's time to break out the note pad again. Think about the navigation first. Do you want the buttons down the side or across the top? Try not to be too weird, while still thinking outside the box. What may seem a wonderful idea as you're designing can be frustrating for visitors; they should find the site intuitive and easy to navigate. Decide where the content will be placed. As a rule of thumb, maximize the content area and try not to take over the whole page with navigation. Flash and pizzazz may look cool at first, but visitors will soon tire of the eye candy and desire to get into the meat of the site.

> **TIP**
>
> Try to avoid making the visitor scroll the page too much, and completely avoid the need to scroll both horizontally and vertically on the same page.

It's now time to make a rough sketch of the site. This step doesn't have to produce anything fancy, since you are just brainstorming at this point. You may create dozens of rough sketches until you decide on a good starting point. Web design brainstorming can look many different ways. One way, what I call the "hit and hope" method, opens up the doors to spontaneity. You begin designing with nothing particular in mind and develop the look as your thoughts progress. In times when your inspirational well seems dry, this experimental method can help open floodgates of possibilities. However, this method can also be slow, as you find that you need to duplicate many tasks—it can be like taking a hike without a map; it may reveal some interesting scenery that you may have never seen before but can also mean you may wander in circles.

The next method usually produces the best results. It involves sketching out some kind of a storyboard (a rough visual of what the page will look like). I like this method because it can give you an idea of where everything will go, and when you open up Photoshop, you can further refine the look. Again, this sketch doesn't have to be fancy—to illustrate, look at Figure 1-2, showing a rough sketch of the home page.

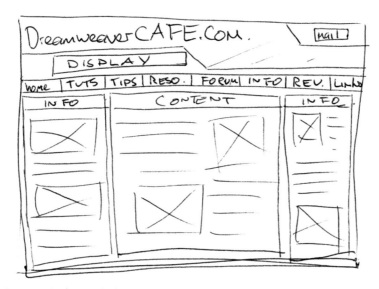

Figure 1–2: The rough sketch

Comp Creation

Once you have finished the wireframe, you'll produce a *comp*—an industry term, short for comprehensive sketch, which is a further rendered and polished sketch of the site that you can show to a client. We will put together the comp in Photoshop. Figure 1-3 shows the finished comp of our sketch. We will create and finesse this comp as we progress through the book.

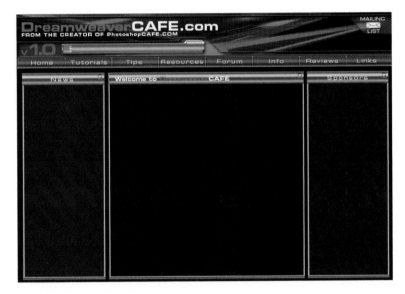

Figure 1–3: Photoshop comp

Pull It All Together

The final step of the wireframe process is to pull together all the components. You should have the following:

- A site map of links and pages
- A sketch of how the main page will look

- A list of all the required assets (which can be difficult to prepare at this point of the project; if so, a partial list will provide a starting point):
  - A list of images required
  - The required copy (text)
  - A list of special items, such as sound and movie clips
  - A list of extra features required, such as forms and any dynamic or interactive content.

PhotoshopCAFE
THE FREE RESOURCE FOR PHOTOSHOP USERS

Contact
Main person: ....
Phone: .... Email: ....
Technical person: ....
Phone: .... Email: ....   Site Map for ....

FTP
URL: ....
User Name: ....
Password: ....
Please check off
☐ **Images**
☐ **Text Files**
☐ **Sound Files**
☐ **50% Payment**
☐ **Other**

NOTES

CHAPTER 2

UNDERSTAND AND USE COLOR AND IMAGERY TO REINFORCE THE MESSAGE

We all love to see great-looking designs, especially because we are designers. But a great design consists of more that just nice aesthetics and the latest Photoshop tricks: a great design communicates a clear message. And because the Web is a medium all about communication, what's the point in creating and using a great design if it is not also functional? Just look at the voting forms for the 2002 American presidential elections for an example of a design that doesn't function too well (remember some confusion about the voting results?). Several factors influence the message that is conveyed in a web page, and the web medium has limitations that designers have to deal with.

TALKING WITH COLOR

A picture is worth 1000 words for sure, and that's why we must make sure that our design is consistent with the message that we are trying to communicate. Otherwise, we will have 1000 "subconscious" words arguing with our written words. Several aspects of a design will influence your message, and one of the strongest of these is the use of color.

Color Anatomy

As far as design is concerned, color is divided into the following three basic parts, as illustrated in Figure 2-1:

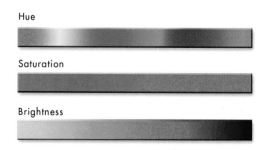

Figure 2–1: Hue, saturation, and brightness.

- **Hue:** The actual color, according to spectral illumination. Look at a rainbow, and you will see the full spectrum of colors: red, orange, yellow, green, blue, indigo, and violet. Every color hue will fall somewhere on this spectrum.

- **Saturation:** The intensity of the color or amount of gray present in a particular hue, sometimes specified as a percentage in the art world.

- **Brightness:** The radiance of a color, affected by the amount of white or black (light) present in a color.

Choosing Colors

A big factor on the "mood" of a color is the color *temperature*. Colors such as orange, red, and yellow are considered *warm* colors. At the opposite end of the spectrum, greens and blues are *cool* colors. This is illustrated in Figure 2-2.

Temperature

Warmer   Cooler

Figure 2–2: Color temperatures.

How does this affect us, you may ask? Consider building a web page for an ice cream company or a ski resort vacation. Cooler colors such as blue would work well, but red would make no sense at all. On the other hand, if you are commissioned to create a design for a tanning studio, the color blue wouldn't work too well as compared to yellow hues.

Each color communicates a different emotion, and that is why it's important to choose colors that work for your design. Here is a brief description of some of the commonly accepted meanings of colors. This list is not exhaustive, and some colors have several meanings.

- **White:** Purity, cleanliness, peace, innocence
- **Black:** Death, sophistication, expense, power, mystery, class
- **Red:** Hot, romance, flash, sex, danger, stop
- **Pink:** Feminine, soft, youthful
- **Orange:** Hot, friendly, energetic
- **Yellow:** Warm, sunny
- **Green:** Cool, new, natural, fresh, go
- **Brown/Beige:** Natural, earthy, classic
- **Blue:** Cool, masculine, serene, wet, dependable, airy
- **Purple:** Cool, royal, spiritual, elegant, rich

Using Photoshop's Color Palette and Color Picker to Create Colors

You select and view color in Photoshop in different ways, usually via the Color palette and Color Picker.

Color Palette

The Color palette can be launched from Photoshop's main menu or by pressing the F6 key. Move the mouse (eyedropper) in the bottom color slider, and click to choose a color, as shown in Figure 2-3.

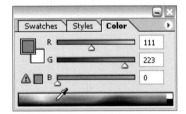

Figure 2–3: Choosing a color in Photoshop's Color palette.

Colors can also be chosen by dragging sliders or entering values into the R, G, and B fields. The color sliders are the color mixers, where you can adjust color by mixing the R (red), G (green), and B (blue) values. As you move a slider to the right, the corresponding amount of the color is added to the mix. The following colors can be created by mixing the R, G, B values shown here:

- Brown: 102, 51, 0
- Purple: 204, 0, 255
- Orange: 255, 125, 0
- Pink: 255, 120, 255

Color Picker

A simpler way of choosing colors is via the Color Picker, which is available by clicking one of colored squares in the upper-left corner of the Color palette or by clicking one of the colored squares in the Toolbox. To use the Color Picker:

1. Choose a hue by moving the Hue slider.

2. Select a tint of the hue (its saturation and brightness value) in the main window by clicking in the Foreground Color area, as shown in Figure 2-4.

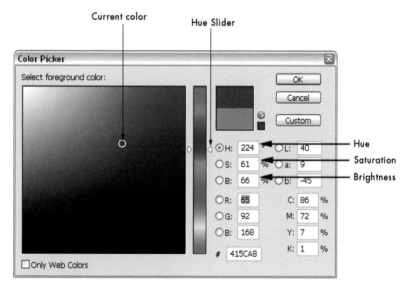

Figure 2–4: Color Picker.

3. Fill out the following fields to create a particular mix of colors.

- **H, S, B:** Hue, saturation, and brightness
- **R, G, B:** Red, green, and blue
- **L, a, b:** Lightness, a and b channels (not used in web)
- **C, M, Y, K:** Cyan, magenta, yellow, and black (used in four-color printing; not used in Web)

Hexadecimal Colors

The field marked with a number sign (#) is called a *hexadecimal* value and is used when you're preparing for web publishing. The hexadecimal value is a six-figure alphanumeric value that specifies a color from the web-safe color palette, discussed next.

> **TIP**
>
> To select any color from an existing image, choose the Eye Dropper tool and click the image.

Web-Safe Colors

A few people are still using color depths of 256 colors on their monitors. However, if your page is using an unsupported color, something called dithering can occur. Dithering causes a pattern of dots that tries to simulate the color used and smoothens transitions between colors. The negative impact with dithering is that it causes patterns of dots to appear in the image. Figure 2-5 shows a color that is dithered.

To combat dithering, and in an attempt to bring some standards in color production, the web-safe palette was conceived. The web-safe palette consists of 216 colors that are shared

Figure 2–5: Dithering.

across different platforms. By using only these colors, you can minimize the effects of dithering. The Color palette in Photoshop and ImageReady can be restricted to use only these 216 web-safe colors; in the Color Picker, click the box labeled Only Web Colors, as shown in Figure 2-6.

Because most peo-
ple are using
equipment that
supports thousands
or millions of col-
ors, you may ask
"Is the web-safe
palette still useful?"
The answer is yes.
Because web-safe
colors are defined
by a hexadecimal
value, they can be

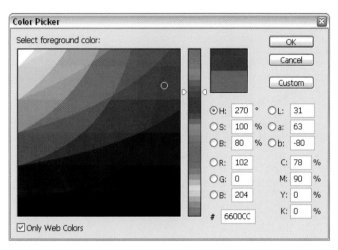

Figure 2–6: Web-safe colors.

faithfully reproduced in HTML. This can be advantageous because large areas of color can be generated in HTML and merged seamlessly with images to cut down on file sizes. A line of code will load much faster than an image on a web page, and every reduction in file size is a good thing. We will explore this concept later in the book as we discuss integration between Photoshop and Dreamweaver.

Building a Color Palette

One of the first things I often do at the beginning of a design project is generate a Color palette. It's a good idea to choose the colors that will be used in a proj-ect and place them in a palette for use. This ensures that the colors are consistent and that they work together, and creating a palette can save you time during the design phase.

Swatches Palette

A quick and consistent way of selecting colors is to click on any of the colored squares (color swatches) inside the Swatches palette to choose a new Foreground color. We can use the Swatches palette to load and store libraries of colors. A number of *libraries* are included with Photoshop, or you can create a custom library. To open the Swatches palette, choose Window | Swatches.

Loading Swatch Libraries

Photoshop comes with a number of color swatches, each containing a library of preset colors. To access these colors, click the arrow at the upper right of the palette, as shown in Figure 2-7. You will see a list of options and palettes.

Choose a color library from the list of options. A dialog box offers three options:

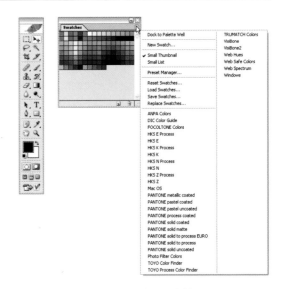

- **OK:** Replaces all the colors with those of the swatch library.

Figure 2-7: Choosing color swatch libraries.

- **Cancel:** Closes the dialog box and cancels loading of a new color swatch.

- **Append:** Adds the colors to the existing colors in the Swatches palette.

Of significance are the Mac OS, Windows, PANTONE, and Web Safe Colors options:

- **Mac OS and Windows:** The system colors of these operating systems.

- **PANTONE:** A color matching system used mainly in printing. Each PANTONE color is assigned a number according to a printed color book. The user can choose a number and be assured that the printed piece will match the color in the color book.

- **Web Safe Colors:** The recommended option for web design, as it contains the 216 web-safe colors.

> **TIP**
>
> To restore the color swatches' factory settings, click the arrow at the top-right of the Swatches palette and choose Reset Swatches.

Adding Custom Colors to the Swatches Palette

You may find it useful to generate a few colors at the beginning of a job and add them to the Color palette for easy access. This ensures that your colors stay consistent throughout the site, and it saves you time by keeping the colors a single click away and minimizing your having to hunt for colors during "design crunch" time.

To add a color to a color swatch, choose the new foreground color from either the Color Picker or the Color palette. Add the color in one of two ways:

- Click the New Swatch icon on the Swatches palette. This icon looks like a piece of paper with one corner folded down.

- Move the mouse into an empty area of the Swatches palette. The cursor will change into a paint bucket containing the current foreground color. Click to add the color. A dialog box will pop up, allowing you to name the color. The current foreground color will be added, as shown in Figure 2-8.

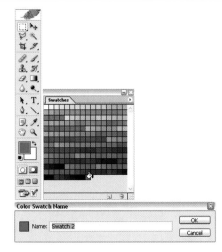

> **TIP**
>
> Double-clicking a color will allow you to change its name after it is included in the swatch library.

Figure 2–8: Adding a color to the palette.

UNDERSTANDING COLOR COMBINATIONS

If you have read the entire chapter to this point, you should now have some understanding of how to create colors in Photoshop. After you choose your web site's main color, you'll need to choose other colors that will appear on the site. But not all colors "go together" well. By choosing harmonious colors that work together, you can make elements blend in or stand out in your design. This is where a little color theory comes in handy. Although you can always "break the rules" to achieve stunning results, you need to be aware of the rules before you can break them.

> **TIP**
>
> Remember if you are using type, its paramount that the text be easy to read.

The Color Wheel

The color wheel displays the primary colors according to their relationship with one another. To make this simple, I have limited this discussion to the three primary colors—red, yellow, and blue—and three secondary colors—orange, green, and purple.

Analogous Colors

One way of choosing colors that work together is to select neighboring colors, or *analogous* colors. If, for example, red is your primary color, then purple and orange are its analogous colors—both orange and purple contain some red, as shown in Figure 2-9. Using these colors can generate moods in color, because they share the same undertones.

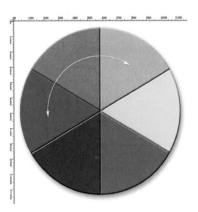

Figure 2–9: Analogous colors.

The colors have an interesting effect the closer they are to each other on the color wheel. Another example of an analogous color combination is yellow and green. Figure 2-10 shows a web page that uses these two colors well.

In many cases, reducing the number of colors on a page can produce a "cleaner" feel, as demonstrated in the two pages shown in Figure 2-11.

Figure 2–10: Colors that are close on the color wheel.

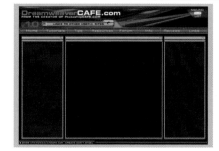

Figure 2–11: Less is more.

Complementary Colors

A complementary color combination involves using colors that are opposite each other on the color wheel, as shown in Figure 2-12.

Using this method produces colors that create a lot of contrast and a balanced sense of color. Examples include the complementary colors red and green that are used for Christmas colors. Another popular combination is orange and blue.

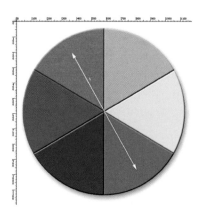

Figure 2–12: Complementary colors.

Figure 2-13 shows an example of how well this combination works. Note that the darker background produces a sense of sophistication.

Figure 2–13: Complementary colors.

Figure 2-14 shows a web site that I designed for a client. I was going for a high-fashion theme, so I used hues of purple with a lot of pink. For an accent, I chose orange. These shades all contain reds and are neighbors on the color wheel, so they work well together.

Figure 2–14: Color use on a fashion web.

CHOOSING A TEXTURE

When creating web pages, color is only one of the choices you must make. You can also spruce things up a bit by using textures. In Figure 2-15, I added some texture to this otherwise colorless entry page. Without the texture, this page would have looked dull and uninteresting—as you can see, a little texture goes a long way.

Figure 2–15: Subtle use of texture can spruce up an entry page.

To create the feel of scratches and texture, I used some custom brushes in Photoshop. You can download brushes from various places on the Internet, including Adobe Exchange, at **http://www.actionxchange.com**.

> **CAUTION**
>
> Be very careful when using textures, as they can greatly reduce readability of text on web pages.

Tiling Backgrounds

In HTML, whenever you assign an image as a background, it will tile (or repeat) indefinitely. A lot of texture can be generated from a small image file using this technique. Because the image repeats, this means that the image has to download only once from the web server. After that, the HTML will repeat the image. This technique has been used by web designers for years. Figure 2–16 shows an example of a tiling (repeating) background.

You can use several strategies to make the most of tiling. In this section, we will look at the process of creating seamless textures in Photoshop. Later in the book, you will implement them in web pages using Dreamweaver.

Figure 2–16: Tiled pattern.

Creating Tiled Backgrounds

As mentioned, when an image is used as a background, it will tile automatically. You can take advantage of this ability by creating backgrounds that are extremely small and tiling them to fill the page. Let's look at an example:

1. Create a new document. In the New document dialog box shown in Figure 2-17, notice the 1600 pixels width setting. Although this is larger than you would usually need, using

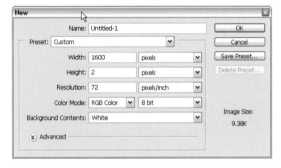

Figure 2–17: The New document dialog box.

this setting makes the screen wide enough so that the pattern will not repeat horizontally on a screen using a horizontal resolution of 1600 pixels or less. Set height to 2 pixels. Obviously, this will be a very small file. Use the RGB Color mode; this is the correct mode for all online images. Click OK when you're done. Note that we are creating a background that will tile vertically; you can also create patterns that tile horizontally or both vertically and horizontally, depending on the effect you are looking for.

2. In the new document, create a selection using the Marquee tool and fill it with a color. The first 200 pixels will now be blue. (Figure 2–18 is zoomed in so you can see the filled selection.)

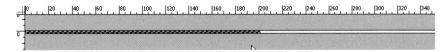

Figure 2–18: Filling a selection with a color.

3. Figure 2-19 shows the finished image. It is very thin, but once we place it in HTML and it tiles, this image will fill the page. Save the image as a GIF or a JPEG. For the purposes of this procedure, name it bg.gif, and save it on your hard drive. You'll be using it in a minute.

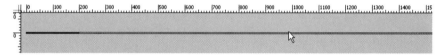

Figure 2–19: Finished background image.

4. At this point in Dreamweaver, choose the image you just created, bg.gif, to use as the background. (We will walk through this in Part III, the Dreamweaver section of this book.)

5. Create a new HTML document in Dreamweaver, and choose Modify | Page Properties.

6. In the Page Properties dialog box, choose the image you created, bg.gif, as the background image—you can locate it on your hard drive by clicking the Browse button, as shown in Figure 2-20.

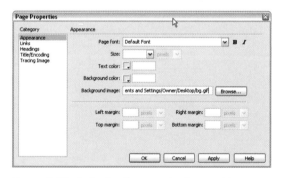

Figure 2–20: Assigning the page background image.

7. Click OK, and then (in Dreamweaver) press the F12 key to preview the page in your web browser.

Figure 2-21 shows our image displayed as a background on a web page. Notice that the image fills the entire page. Background images will tile both horizontally and vertically. They can be applied to the entire page or to tables or cells.

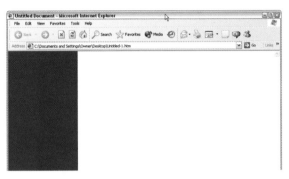

Figure 2–21: Tiled background.

Creating Seamless Backgrounds

You are not limited to a solid color for a background. For example, you could create a custom texture or even use a photograph for your background. Figure 2-22 shows a texture created as a tile using the Texturizer filter in Photoshop. To access this filter, choose Filter | Texture | Texturizer.

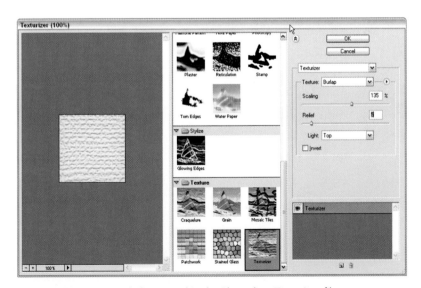

Figure 2–22: A textured tile created in the Photoshop Texturizer filter.

When tiling an image, sometimes the edges don't quite match and the seams between tiles can show. In Figure 2-23, you can see where the tiles repeat—in most cases, this is very undesirable.

You can prepare textures so that they will repeat seamlessly—they just need a little touching up on the edges.

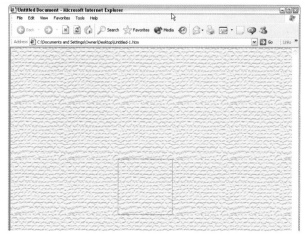

Figure 2–23: The seams are visible on this tile (one tile is outlined in red for reference).

1. With the texture open in Photoshop, choose Filter | Other | Offset.

2. In the Offset filter dialog box, choose a Horizontal setting of 15, a Vertical setting of 15, and select the Wrap Around radio button, as shown in Figure 2-24. This shifts the image down and to the right by 15 pixels, which is just enough to see the seam in the image window. Click OK.

3. Choose the Clone Stamp tool from the Toolbox. You'll use this tool to blend the seams and make them disappear.

4. Hold down the ALT (OPTION) key and click a similar section of the image that is not a seam. The cursor will turn into a

Figure 2–24: Using the Offset filter.

crosshair. You can now sample a section of the image.

5. Click and drag the mouse to paint with the selected texture. Paint away the seams, as shown in Figure 2-25.

6. Now that the seams have been repaired, return the image to its original position. Choose Filter | Other | Offset.

7. This time, choose the opposite settings in the Offset filter dialog box: –15 and –15 for Horizontal and Vertical. This will restore the image to its original position, as shown in Figure 2-26. This time, the edges of the tiles will blend because you just fixed them with the Clone Stamp tool.

8. Now tile the same image, and look at Figure 2-27 to see how much smoother it looks. The seams are now gone.

Figure 2–25: Using the Clone Stamp tool to "repair" the seams.

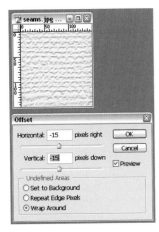

Figure 2–26: Returning the image to its original position.

Figure 2–27: Tiling the repaired image.

> **CAUTION**
>
> Be sure to use color and texture wisely, remembering that everything you add
> to the page should strengthen the message. Do not use too much color or too
> much texture; overusing these elements can make the page look busy, crowd-
> ed, and difficult to look at and read the information.

CHOOSING IMAGES

When you choose images for your web site, think about the meaning of the
images. Try to resist the temptation to add something just because it looks cool.
Remember that if the words "spoken" by the images, colors, textures, and the web
page text don't match well, it causes an "argument," and the page will look very
noisy. I don't know about you, but if people are arguing, I quickly leave the scene.
Your visitors will do the same thing!

When selecting images, look for colors and shapes that work with your web site
and intended product or service. Try to use images that provoke an emotional
response. People are moved by art, and you can communicate with viewers by
choosing appropriate art. Try to spark an emotion or a memory so that the viewer will identify with the web page. So often, young web designers know how to
spark only one emotion: "Wow!" This can be great, but if you want to sell products or establish a company's brand, it's going to take more that just a wow.

Take a look at the U.S. Air Force web site in Figure 2-28, which uses images of
people and families. This creates a stronger emotional connection than merely fea-
turing images of aircraft. Notice also the strong use of blue, which conveys
dependability and security.

Figure 2-28: Good use of strong imagery.

CHAPTER 3

DESIGN THE INTERFACE AND NAVIGATION

This chapter looks at techniques for designing a user interface, such as navigation buttons and other elements that appear in web page layouts created in Photoshop. We will look at a few tricks that you can use to add visual punch to your web page layouts.

I'll show you step-by-step how I built my DreamweaverCAFE.com splash screen in Photoshop. As you work through the processes outlined here, you are encouraged to develop your own design ideas and use what you learn in this chapter as a guideline. Don't be glued to the design ideas that are used here; instead, adapt what you learn to your own web page designs. Be creative! Although most web pages' basic elements—such as navigation bars and content areas—are similar, you should try to create a unique look based on your own imagination and what you have learned so far.

CREATING A NEW DOCUMENT

The first question you may ask is, "How big should I make my page?" The page should be large enough to accommodate your content, but small enough to fit on an average viewer's computer screen. Obviously, if the page is too large to be displayed, important portions of your content or navigation would be hidden from the user. It's quite common for the user to scroll through the content vertically, but making a user scroll vertically and horizontally is a big no-no. Typical screen resolutions will vary, but 1024-768 is the most commonly used resolution for web pages.

HOW DIFFERENT SCREEN RESOLUTIONS DISPLAY IMAGES

As screen resolutions get higher, contents appear smaller. The following illustration shows how the same page would appear using different screen resolutions.

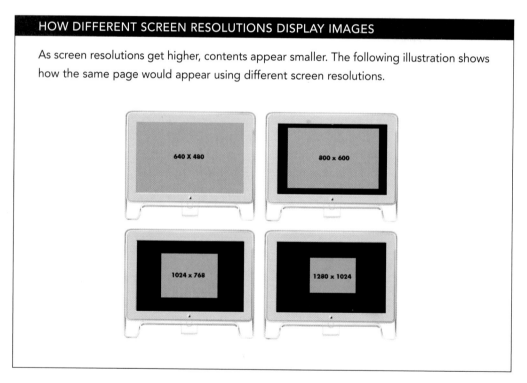

At this point, it's a good idea to design for a minimum screen resolution of 800x600, because a lot of people are still using older computers and others may have poor eyesight; dropping the resolution to about that size makes your page readable for everyone. Remember that you need to leave room for the web browser's interface—that leaves the ideal starting resolutions setting at 775x550 pixels, which should be fully visible on a monitor set to 800x600 resolution. Remember that you can always change the height of the page later as you are building the content.

CREATING THE LAYOUT IN PHOTOSHOP

Let's create our comp design in Photoshop. This will be a design that is still a little rough and not yet functional. Comps are used to get client approval of the aesthetic design before building the entire site. It's much quicker to make a change to a Photoshop document than to an entire HTML page. (In design parlance, a comp is short for composition.)

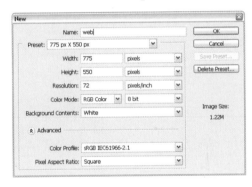

1. Create a new document by choosing File | New. In the New dialog box, use the settings shown in Figure 3-1.

Figure 3–1: New document settings for a web page.

2. This step is optional. If you have created a pencil or pen sketch of the page, such as the one shown in Figure 3-2, scan it into your computer and place it inside the new document. This will give you a rough template from which to work.

Figure 3–2: Sketch scanned into Photoshop.

3. Set up your guides, as shown in Figure 3-3. These guides mark the header, navigation, and content areas of the site. Of course, if you use a different layout—one with a side navigation area, for example—this will look a little different. Press CTRL-R (CMD-R on the Mac) to show rulers. Drag the guides from the rulers to create them.

Figure 3–3: Setup guides.

4. Now let's create the header area's background. Use your artistic freedom here and create a header image—it could be as simple as a solid color, a photograph, or a custom design like the one I used in Figure 3-4. The best advice at this point is to keep it simple. I've added a gray bar to demarcate the header area of the content. (You'll see how to add lines to a page later in the chapter in the section "Creating Inset Lines.")

Figure 3–4: A header area background image.

5. Choose the Rectangular shape tool from the Tools palette. Create a new layer and then drag to select the area you want to use for the navigation area, where the navigation buttons will be placed.

6. To fill the layer, make a selection and fill with a solid color, as shown in Figure 3-5. I've used a gray color here.

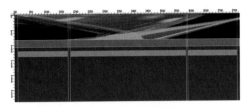

Figure 3–5: Assign the navigation area.

7. Use the Rectangular shape tool, create another new layer, and draw a rectangle to represent each of the columns that will be filled with content, such as text. For Figure 3-6, I chose the Fill pixel option on the Options bar to use pixels rather than paths. Drag the shape tool to create the columns in the content area, using the guides to assist you.

Fill pixel option

Rectangular shape tool

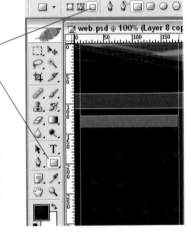

Figure 3–6: Define the content area.

Figure 3-7 shows the basic layout of the web page. Next, we'll build out each element and add navigation.

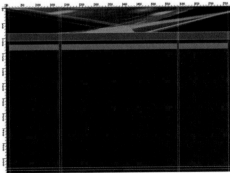

Figure 3–7: Basic layout

CREATING THE NAVIGATION

Users click buttons, text, or icons to move around a web site. In this example, we will create some buttons to use for navigation.

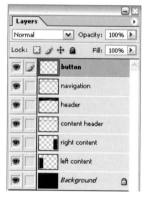

Figure 3–8: The Layers palette.

1. In the Layers palette create a new layer, and name it **button**. Figure 3-8 shows the Layers palette so far in this project. Notice how each of the key elements is named on its own layer.

2. Now it's time to do a little easy math. We need to decide how many navigation buttons we want to add to the site—for DreamweaverCAFE, we used eight buttons. Since the width of the navigation area is 775 pixels, divide 775 by 8 to create eight evenly spaced and sized buttons across the page. Our calculation shows that 775/8 = 96.875 pixels; because we can't deal with fractions of a pixel, round the size up to 97 pixels. (Always round up; if you round down, you will be left with ugly gaps in your design. Also, if you created a side navigation area, you would divide the height, rather than the width, by the number of buttons to see how tall the buttons would need to be.) The height of the navigation bar area is 25 pixels. So we know that the size of each button should be 97x25 pixels.

3. Choose File | New, and in the New dialog box, type in the name button. Use

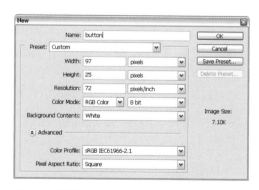

Figure 3–9: The settings for the new button.

the settings shown in Figure 3-9. Click OK when you're done.

4. In the new document, create a new layer and fill it with either a solid color or a gradient. Figure 3-10 shows that a black to green linear gradient is used.

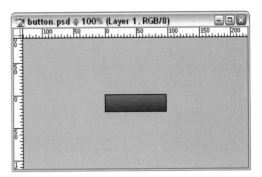

Figure 3–10: The beginning of the new button.

5. Now we'll add some depth and create a ridge around the button. Create a new layer.

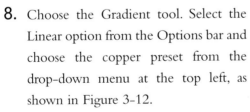

Figure 3–11: Making the selection.

6. Using the Rectangular marquee tool, select the new button, as shown in Figure 3-11.

7. You can see that the center area of the button is selected; however, we want to select the edges of the button so we can add some effects there, so we will invert the selection. Choose Select | Inverse.

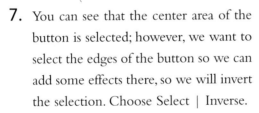

Figure 3–12: Choosing the copper gradient preset.

8. Choose the Gradient tool. Select the Linear option from the Options bar and choose the copper preset from the drop-down menu at the top left, as shown in Figure 3-12.

9. Drag the gradient diagonally through the button to add the copper to its outside rim, as shown in Figure 3-13.

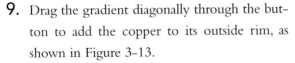

Figure 3–13: Adding the gradient.

10. Press CTRL-D (CMD-D) to turn off the selection.

11. Press CTRL-SHIFT-U (CMD-SHIFT-U) to desaturate the color as shown in Figure 3–14. This gives us a metallic looking result.

Figure 3–14: Desaturating the color on the button's rim.

12. Now let's add a bevel to the rim of the button to complete the depth. Click the Layer Styles button from the bottom of the Layers palette (it looks like an *f*).

13. In the Layer Style window that opens, select a bevel style and use the other settings shown in Figure 3–15.

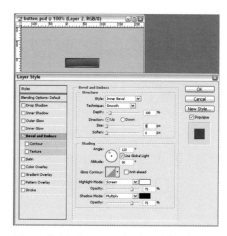

Figure 3–15: Creating the bevel for the button's rim.

Creating a Glassy Button

Now we'll give the button a glassy gloss.

1. Create a new layer and type glass as its name in the Layers palette, as shown in Figure 3–16.

2. Move this layer beneath the rim layer (which is named layer 2).

3. Choose white as the foreground color.

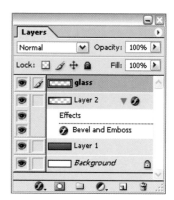

Figure 3–16: Creating the new layer.

4. Choose the Linear gradient tool and select the foreground to transparent option, as shown in Figure 3-17.

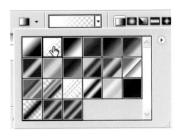

Figure 3–17: Selecting the foreground to transparent gradient.

5. Create the gradient starting from the top of the button to about halfway down. When you're done, it should look like the button shown in Figure 3-18.

6. In the Layers palette, set the Opacity of the gradient to 64 percent.

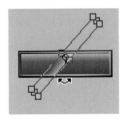

Figure 3–18: Applying the gradient.

7. Duplicate the glass layer.

8. Choose the Free transform tool by pressing CTRL-T (CMD-T).

9. Position the Move tool outside one of the transform box corners until it turns into a curved arrow.

10. Click and drag to rotate the gradient 180 degrees, as shown in Figure 3-19.

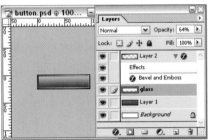

Figure 3–19: Rotating the gradient.

11. Position the rotated gradient at the bottom of the button, and lower the Opacity setting in the Layers palette to 35 percent, as shown in Figure 3-20. You now have a glassy looking button with metallic edges.

Figure 3–20: Repositioning the duplicated gradient to complete the effect.

CREATING AN AQUA GEL BUTTON

A popular type of button often used on web pages is the aqua gel button, which looks
a bit like the type of button used on the Mac interface.

1. Create a new document. Make it 97x25 pixels in size.

2. Choose the Rounded rectangle tool, as shown in Figure 3-21.

3. In the Options bar, choose the Radius, Mode, and Opacity settings shown in Figure 3-22.

Figure 3–21: Rounded rectangle tool.

Figure 3–22: Setting the options.

4. Create a new layer.

5. Click and drag to create a pill-shaped, or rounded rectangle shaped, button, as shown in Figure 3-23.

Figure 3–23: Drawing a button.

6. Press CTRL (CMD) and click the layer thumbnail—you will see the "marching ants" appear around the button, indicating that it has been selected.

7. Fill the button with a dark to light blue gradient, like the one shown in Figure 3-24.

Figure 3–24: Filling the gradient.

8. With the selection still active, create a new layer.

9. Choose a white to transparent gradient and apply it to the top half of the button.

Figure 3–25:
Free transform with
the new white to
transparent gradient.

10. Press CTRL-T (CMD-T). This will show some bounding boxes for Free transform mode, as shown in Figure 3-25. This allows us to rotate scale and otherwise transform our layer.

11. Click and drag on the button's side handles; bring in each of the sides and the top and bottom just a little bit, as shown in Figure 3-26. (This will add to the illusion of a rounded shape.)

Figure 3–26:
Adjusting the gradient.

12. Press the ENTER (RETURN) key to apply the transformation. Press CTRL-D (CMD-D) to turn off the selection.

13. Choose Filter | Blur | Gaussian Blur, and in the Gaussian Blur dialog box, set the Radius to about 1.4, as shown in Figure 3-27. This will soften the edges of the highlight. Then click OK.

Figure 3–27: Blurring the gradient.

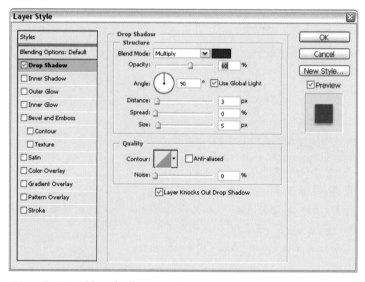

Figure 3–28: Adding the layer style for a drop shadow.

14. Finally, add a drop shadow layer effect. Select the pill-shaped layer (beneath the glass layer). Click the Layer Styles button to open the Layer Style window and select Drop Shadow from the Styles area. Choose dark blue for the color and lower the Opacity setting to 60 percent. Change the Angle to 90 degrees, as shown in Figure 3-28. Experiment with the Distance slider to achieve the desired effect.

We have finished the gel button, which is shown in Figure 3-29.

Figure 3–29:
The gel button.

CREATING A TABBED BUTTON

Another popular type of navigation is the tabbed button. You can see how these are used at **http://www.apple.com**. ImageReady CS has made it easier than ever to create this type of button.

1. Open ImageReady (installed with Photoshop) and choose the Tab rectangle tool, as shown in Figure 3-30. If you want, you can change the radius of the curve in the Options bar later on.

2. Click and drag to create a single tab, as shown in Figure 3-31.

3. You can jazz up the tab a bit if you want by using layer styles or by using the techniques already shown in this chapter.

Figure 3–30: Choosing the Tab rectangle tool.

Figure 3–31: Creating the tab.

Adding the Buttons to the Main Page

After you've created a button, the next step is to add it to your web page. Save your button document as a layered PSD file if you haven't already done so. To simplify things, we are going to flatten the layers of the buttons. You may also choose to arrange the layered buttons into a layer set and work with them that way. If you have created a button directly on the web page document, you can skip these steps.

1. Open your button document or create one now. Save the file. Hide the background by turning off the Background layer in the Layers palette.

2. Choose Merge, visible from the drop-down menu at the top right of the Layers palette.

Figure 3–32: Adding a button to the main page.

3. Click and drag the button onto your main web page and position it similarly to the button shown in Figure 3-32.

4. Close the button document without saving again so that you preserve the layers in case you need them later.

Duplicating and Aligning Elements on a Page

We are now going to take advantage of the alignment and distribution tools in Photoshop, which will save us some work and produce pinpoint accuracy.

1. To duplicate the button, choose its layer in the Layers palette, hold down the ALT (OPTION) key, and drag the button. You will notice that you are dragging a copy of the button, as shown in Figure 3-33. If you also hold down the SHIFT key, the drag movement will be constrained to a straight line.

Figure 3–33: Dragging a copy of the button.

2. Continue dragging copies until you have created all

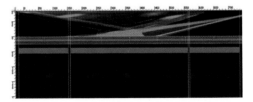

Figure 3-34: All the buttons on the navigation bar.

eight buttons that you need for the web page's navigation bar, as shown in Figure 3-34. Don't worry too much about perfect placement as you're dragging copies. We'll fix that next.

3. Make sure the placement of the first and last buttons is correct.

4. Link all the buttons together in the Layers palette, as shown in Figure 3-35.

5. Select the Move tool, and the Align and Distribute tools will appear in the Options bar (see Figure 3-36).

6. Choose the Top Align button to use for the top navigation buttons (or choose the Left Align button for side navigation buttons).

7. Click the Distribute Center Horizontal button to fix the spacing on the buttons along the top navigation bar, as shown in Figure 3-36. (For side navigation, choose Distribute Center Vertical.)

8. The buttons should now be positioned correctly. If the whole navigation bar is slightly off where you want it to appear, just tap the arrow keys on your keyboard to nudge the linked buttons.

Figure 3-35: Buttons linked.

Figure 3-36: Distributing the layers.

9. Now we'll add some labels for the buttons, as shown in Figure 3-37. Labels are text that identify the link. Create each label on its own layer and use the Align and Distribute tools in the Options bar to align the text.

Figure 3–37: Adding the text labels.

> **TIP**
>
> When adding text labels, use a clean and readable font such as Arial or Futura. Also, set the tracking (space between letters) wider than normal to increase readability at smaller font sizes.

ADDING "EYE CANDY" TO THE PAGE

The following steps are optional, and you probably don't want every web page you create to include similar elements or your pages will all look the same. Remember that this example site is just one design out of limitless possibilities. This section discussed the techniques I used in the DreamweaverCAFE site so that you can understand how it all came together. Feel free to use these techniques and apply them to your own pages, but try to create something unique—make it personalized and make it your own.

CREATING COOL PATTERNS FOR THE INTERFACE

You will notice that in the DreamweaverCAFE design, I have used some patterns to embellish the interface. These patterns are fairly easy to create and are added to the pattern library. You can download a pattern set from the book's web site at **http://www.dreamweavercafe.com/book**.

Here's how you can create some of these patterns:

1. Create a new document. Make it 2x2 pixels and choose a white background.

2. Zoom in on the document at 1600 percent so that you can work on the four pixels.

3. Choose the Pencil tool, set it to a single pixel wide, and use black as the foreground color.

4. Fill the top two pixels with black so that the top half of the document is black and the bottom half is white.

5. Choose Select | All. The entire 4-pixel image should be selected.

6. Choose Edit | Define Pattern. Provide a name for the pattern: let's use scan-line.

The pattern is now added to the library and available for use from the Fill menu or Patterns in the Layer Styles.

For a variation, try making a 2x2 pixel document and fill it with white. Make the top left and the bottom right pixels black; this will create a pixel grid pattern that can also look great. To make the pattern larger, create a larger document and use thicker lines. Patterns can also be created in color.

Creating the Illusion of Depth

Let's focus again on the header area of the page; I want to add some depth to the page to make it look like a 3D object that people can touch. The following techniques will help to achieve this end:

1. Choose the Polygon Lasso tool from the Tools palette, as shown in Figure 3–38.

    The Polygon Lasso tool is used to make selections that consist of straight lines that surround the selected object or objects. This tool is ideal for creating the modern "interface" look that is so popular. Here's how to use the tool:

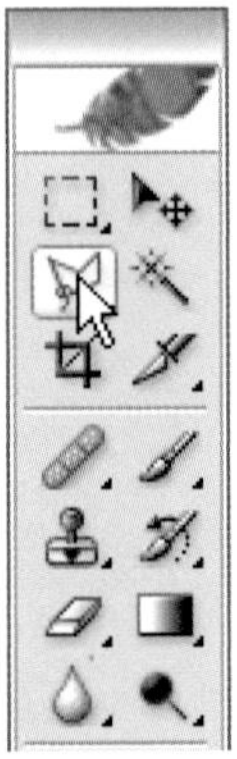

2. Click a point where you want to begin your selection.

3. Click again somewhere else and the two points will be joined. Each time you click, a new line is drawn to connect the new point to the last one. To finish drawing and close the selection lasso, move the cursor over the starting point. When a small circle appears, click to complete the selection. The "marching ants" will appear to indicate the selected area, as shown in Figure 3–39. The selection I created in Figure 3–39 is fairly complex; yours can be simpler if you prefer.

Figure 3–38: Polygon Lasso tool.

Figure 3–39: A selection in the header area.

TIP

Hold down the SHIFT key to constrain the Polygon Lasso tool to vertical lines, horizontal lines, and 45-degree angles.

4. Create a new layer and fill it with a solid color. I used black in Figure 3-40, but the color can always be changed later if necessary.

Figure 3–40: Filling the selection.

5. Now we'll create the depth to the interface. We will attach a layer style to the shape to give it the illusion of being recessed into the header. Click the Add a Layer Style button at the bottom left of the Layers palette. The Layer Style dialog box will open.

6. Choose the Bevel And Emboss style from the Styles list.

7. From the Style drop-down list in the Structure area, choose Pillow Emboss. Use the settings shown in Figure 3-41.

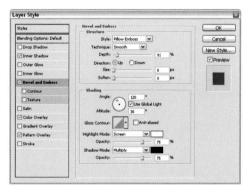

Figure 3–41: Bevel settings.

8. Add an inner shadow effect. Click Inner Shadow from the Styles list. The settings used in Figure 3-42 will create a recessed look.

9. Let's change the base color to green. Click Color Overlay in the Styles list and select a color that matches your design. Notice in Figure 3-43 that the Opacity setting has been lowered to 37 percent; this allows other elements to show through the header area.

Figure 3–42: Inner shadow effect.

10. This step is optional. I have chosen a Pattern Overlay for the header area using the scan-line pattern that we created earlier in the chapter, in the section "Creating Cool Patterns for the Interface", as shown in Figure 3-44. This will create a seamless repeating pattern on the layer. Choose the pattern from the window that provides access to the pattern library.

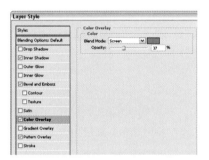

Figure 3–43: Choosing a new base color.

11. In the Layer Style dialog box, click OK to apply the layer style. Figure 3-45 shows how the new layer adds a lot of depth and zing to the header area of our page.

Figure 3–44: Pattern overlay.

Figure 3–45: The interface with a recessed header.

CREATING INSET LINES

A great way to add depth and a 3D look to a page is a technique called inset lines, which creates lines with a 3D look to them. Here's how it's done:

1. Create a new layer.

2. Using the Line tool (nested with the shape tools in the toolbar). Choose White for the color and 1 pixel from the Options bar. Then choose the 3. Fill pixel option (shown back in Figure 3-6).

Figure 3–46:
A straight line.

3. SHIFT-click and drag to draw a horizontal line, shown in Figure 3-46.

4. In the Layers palette, duplicate the line layer, which is Layer 1. A new layer called Layer 1 Copy will appear, as shown in Figure 3-47.

Figure 3–47: Duplicate the line.

5. Press CTRL-I (CMD-I) to invert the line copy's color to black, as shown in Figure 3-48.

6. Press the up arrow key on the keyboard once to nudge the line up a single pixel. Notice that the line now appears three dimensional, as shown in Figure 3-49.

Figure 3–48: Inverted color on the line.

TIP

To create a thicker line, increase the size of the line, but remember to nudge the copy by only a single pixel to achieve the desired result.

Figure 3–49:
The inset line.

Using the techniques learned so far, finish up the web page. Add logos, headers, and some inset lines to jazz things up a bit. Notice that I used the inset line technique and some gradients to make the content areas look a bit better. Your page should now be looking similar to what you envisioned when you created the sketch in the first chapter. The almost finished DreamweaverCAFE page is shown in Figure 3-50.

Figure 3–50: The almost finished DreamweaverCAFE page design.

ADDING A SECONDARY ROLLOVER INTERFACE

When the mouse rolls over a button, a secondary rollover causes more than one change to occur on the page. For example, when you roll over a navigation button on DreamweaverCAFE.com, the button changes color and a small display screen above the buttons displays some text that provides a description of the page that you will be transported to if you click the button. Here's how you can create a similar display:

1. Create a new layer.

2. Using the Polygon Lasso tool, create the shape of the text display. I used a thin, horizontal rectangle, but you can make it any shape you want.

3. Fill the shape with a gradient, as shown in Figure 3-51 (refer to the online help in Photoshop if you do not know how to create a custom gradient).

Figure 3–51: The shape filled with a custom gradient.

You will notice in Figure 3-52 that I created a fancy end cap for the display. This is not that hard; it's just two rectangular selections, one filled with a gradient and the other using the scan line pattern.

Figure 3–52: A custom end cap.

4. Now create a metal enclosure for the screen, as shown in Figure 3-53. First, I loaded the selection from the Display shape. Then I created a new layer

Figure 3–53: The final display area interface.

and filled it with the copper gradient (see the earlier "Creating the Glassy Button" section; this is very similar). I then used the Rectangular marquee tool to make a selection and then deleted it to cut out the center of the metal layer. Finally, I desaturated the copper gradient to achieve the steel look.

Figure 3–54: The custom text.

5. Now create the custom text to be displayed, as shown in Figure 3-54.

6. Finally, create a line of custom text for each of the buttons. Place each piece of text on its own layer, as shown in Figure 3-55. Hide these text layers for now; we will use them in the next chapter.

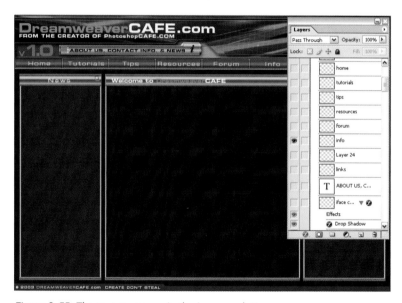

Figure 3–55: The text messages in the Layers palette.

We have completed the web page design, and the finished design is shown in Figure 3-56. We will make it all begin to work in the next couple of chapters.

In the web design world, we now have what is known as a comp. None of the user interface elements work, but the basic layout and design is finished enough to show to a client for approval. Remember that it's much easier to make design changes now than it will be after the page is sliced up and converted to HTML. You can also make up some rough "dummy" content to show the client how the page might look when it's finished.

Figure 3–56: The finished web page design.

PART II

PREPARE THE FILES FOR THE WEB

CHAPTER 4

CREATE IMAGE MAPS AND ROLLOVERS WITH SLICES

You've planned how your site will look and created a visual comp in Photoshop that looks like the real page. At this point, however, it's still lacking functionality. In this chapter, we'll begin turning the comp into a working web page. This chapter focuses on slicing an image and creating tables to contain and separate information. Although you may not need to use slices and tables for every web site you create, you'll find the information in this chapter helpful in the future as you develop various kinds of pages. You'll also learn how to create image maps, rollovers, and remote rollovers so you can add interactivity and some "wow factor" to your web pages. The information in this chapter covers the first steps in turning a comp layout into a functioning web page.

SLICING BASICS

Assuming you have presented your design to the client and he or she is satisfied with it, it's time to turn your comp into a functioning site. If you were to put your image on the Web as a single, large image, you would face several problems:

- The page would take a long time to load

- The page would be a static site because you haven't added interactivity

- The page would be difficult to update without replacing the entire page

In essence, what you have created is a visual model, not unlike those fake TV sets that furniture stores use to stage a scene—it looks like the real thing, but pick it up and it becomes apparent that it's quite impossible to watch anything. The solution is to break the image into smaller parts—to slice it using the Slice tool in Photoshop or ImageReady—and add functionality to the different parts, which we'll call *zones*.

> **NOTE**
>
> To simplify this discussion, I came up with the term *zone* system. I'm sure others use something similar, though they may use a different name.

The Zone System

The zone system boils down to this: Rather than approach the page as a whole and attempt to slice it, it is better to think in *zones* first, such as the navigation, header, and content zones. I have found that many people have struggled with the concept of slicing and I believe that the zone system is the solution.

First we will divide the page into zones; then we will slice and optimize each zone independently. This way, the task is simplified and produces better results that are easy to work with later on. Three main zones appear in the average web page:

- **Header:** Identifies to whom the web site belongs
- **Navigation:** Suggests how the visitor navigates around the site
- **Content:** Provides visitors with information you want them to read

Although you may never need to update the navigation and header zones for your site, if a successful web page is the goal, the content should be updated regularly. A site may be structured in many different ways, but without these three main elements, it would be pretty pointless. Of course, the zones don't have to be elaborate—a navigation zone could be as simple as a single button, or multiple navigation zones could be used. See Figure 4-1.

Figure 4–1: Navigation zones.

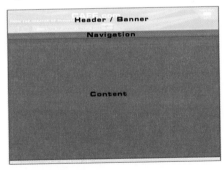
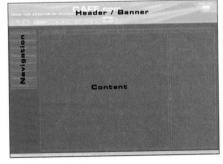

A. Top navigation.

B. Side navigation.

What Is Slicing?

Before the slicing tools in Photoshop were available, the process of creating slices in a web page was complicated: I would begin with a single image and create guides where I wanted to partition the image. Then I would make a selection, crop the image, save the image, and then immediately choose Undo. I would crop a different portion of the image and save that. Once all the parts of the image had been saved, I'd create an HTML table on a new page. Then I'd create the correct number of cells in the table to accommodate the images, insert the images into the table, and then size the table correctly so that the seams would be invisible.

If you consider how slicing was accomplished before the Slice tool was available, you'll really appreciate how easy the Slice tool makes creating zones in a web page.

> **NOTE**
>
> Technically, we are not actually creating separate slices; rather, we are *defining* them by marking the image with slice border definitions. These slice definitions are telling ImageReady to "cut here and make this a separate image, name it, and then arrange it in a new table along with the other images that we are creating."

The Slice tool tells Photoshop where the cuts should be located. When we export an image as HTML (see Chapter 5), each slice will become a separate, smaller image. All these slices will be arranged in tables that will be generated automatically, as shown in Figures 4–2A and 4–2B.

Figure 4–2: Slices arranged in tables.

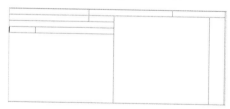

A. The table on its own that holds the images.

B. Sliced images inside a table.

A table is divided into partitions called *cells*. A table consists of a minimum of one cell and has no physical limit (of course, there are practical limits). Each slice is placed inside its own cell. The goal is to produce a functional page with the minimum number of cells to get the job done. Thus, we will try to cut down on the number of slices as much as is practical.

Tables generated in Photoshop are not unlike the tables you create in a spreadsheet. Tables are placed on the page in a web site so that all the pieces are arranged cleanly, touching each other's borders so that the border seams are not visible and the tables appear as a single image, as shown in Figure 4-3.

Figure 4–3: The seamlessly sliced page in a web browser.

Slicing Strategies

Before you start slicing, you need to have a plan that answers such questions as "Where should you add a slice and why?" Here are some suggestions of what you can do:

- Attach functionality to different slices, such as buttons and rollovers (which you'll learn how to create later in this chapter).

- Optimize each slice differently, thus making the page load faster while maintaining the best appearance overall.

- Switch out individual slices instead of the entire page. This allows you to create zones that can be reproduced on several pages. This also allows you to reuse images, which will speed up the page's download time.

- Create rollover effects that need slices to work.

- Create slices around areas that will be changed or replaced, such as a web banner.

- Create a separate section of solid color that can be replaced by HTML or a pattern (covered in Chapter 5).

- Define an area that will be converted to HTML text.

- Separate the text so you can make it look better during optimization (more on this in Chapter 5).

CREATE YOUR FIRST SLICE

Let's create a simple slice right now to help you grasp the concept. If you are familiar with how slicing works, you can skip this tutorial and go to the next section, "Select and Modify Slices."

Figure 4-4 shows an image that has been divided into two zones: header and content. Presently, this is a layered Photoshop image, and we want to slice it and convert it into HTML. You can create a simple image in Photoshop or ImageReady if you want to follow along. Don't worry about how great it looks for now.

Figure 4-4: Image to be sliced.

1. Choose the Slice tool from either Photoshop or ImageReady.

Figure 4–5: Defining a slice.

2. Click and drag with the Slice tool, as you would with the Marquee tool, to define the slice, as shown in Figure 4-5.

TIP

Life is easier if you create guides and choose View | Snap To | Guides before you create slices. To create guides, choose View | Rulers. Click and drag the mouse out of the rulers; guides will appear automatically. Release the mouse to apply the guides.

Notice a small box with a number on the upper left of each slice in Figure 4-6. Photoshop/ImageReady assigns a unique number to each slice so you can identify it. (See the sidebar "Slice Icons" for details.)

As you create a slice, Photoshop or ImageReady will automatically assign slices to the rest of the image to make the new slice work. These slices are called *auto slices*. Whenever you make changes to a slice, the auto slices adjust automatically.

Figure 4–6: Slices shown in ImageReady.

SELECT AND MODIFY SLICES

You'll use the Slice Select tool to select and work with slices. (In ImageReady, you'll find the Slice Select tool next to the Slice tool. In Photoshop, it's located under the Slice tool.) Use this tool to do one or more of the following:

- Click inside a slice to make it the currently active slice.

- Click and drag to reposition a slice.

- Click the edge of a slice and drag it to change the size, as shown in Figure 4-7.

Figure 4-7: Changing the size of a slice.

> **TIP**
>
> You can convert an auto slice to a user slice by selecting it and choosing Promote To User Slice from the Options bar in Photoshop, or by selecting Slices-Promote To User Slice from the Slices menu in ImageReady.

EXPORT A SLICE TO HTML

Let's quickly skim over exporting so you can see the slices. Exporting is covered in more depth in Chapter 5.

To export the sliced image to HTML:

1. In ImageReady, choose File | Save Optimized. (Choose File | Save For Web in Photoshop.)

2. Name the slice files test_01.gif and test_02.gif.

3. Choose the location to which you want to save the files.

4. Click OK.

5. Take a look at your disk and you will notice two files that have been created:

- An HTML document that contains your image table

- A folder called images

6. Open the images folder and view the slices. Figure 4–8 shows the two slices you created.

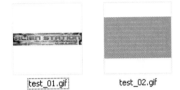

test_01.gif   test_02.gif

Figure 4–8: Individual images as slices.

Hopefully, you have grasped the concept of slicing, which is a very important concept that you will need to grasp in this book. If you are still confused, go back over this section. Now let's move on with our web project.

SLICE ICONS

Whenever a slice is created, an icon will appear on the upper left of the slice. Each of these icons tells you particular information about the slice.

- **User Slice:** A slice that is created manually.

- **Auto Slice:** A slice that was created automatically by Photoshop or ImageReady.

- **Layer Based Slice:** A slice that is based on the boundaries of a layer object.

- **Rollover attached:** This slice will interact with the mouse.

- **Rollover Modified State:** A modified state is selected, such as rollover.

SLICING YOUR PROJECT

Open your design project in ImageReady, if it isn't already open. Let's start slicing your working project. This section covers the zoning for both top- and side-navigation designs to provide you with the skills you need to create any type of site.

First, we'll separate the site's zones with some guides, which will help us create more accurate slices. When the Snap To Guides option is turned on (under the View menu), the cursor will be drawn to a guide whenever it comes within a few pixels of the guide.

To create the guides:

1. In ImageReady, turn on the rulers by pressing CTRL-R (CMD-R on the Mac).

2. Click and hold your mouse anywhere within the rulers and drag toward the document. A new guide will appear.

3. Release the mouse button wherever you want the guide to appear.

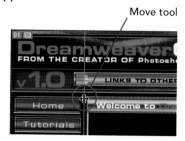

Figure 4–9: Adjusting a guide.

Using the Move tool, you can click and drag a guide to adjust its position on the page, as shown in Figure 4-9. To remove a guide, place the cursor on the guide until it turns into a double arrow. Drag it back into the ruler.

CREATE SLICES FROM THE GUIDES

To create slices along the guides, choose Slices | Create Slices From Guides in ImageReady. The image will be sliced along the guides. The side-navigation page contains six slices, each with a slice number assigned in the upper-left corner, as shown in Figure 4-10.

Figure 4–10: The zones sliced.

COMBINE SLICES

The zones are now nicely sliced in the top navigation design and you don't have to do anything else to your design until the section on tables. It's advisable to continue reading for the sake of learning.

In the case of the side navigation design, there are more slices created than we need. In our page the header and footer each contain two slices and we want them to be a single slice each at this stage. Apply this technique to remove the extra slices on the image.

To combine the slices:

1. In ImageReady, choose the Select Slice tool to select the first slice that you want to work with (slice 01).

2. Hold down the SHIFT key and click slice 02.

3. Slices 01 and 02 should now be selected, as shown in Figure 4–11.

Figure 4–11: Two slices selected for the header.

4. Right-click (CONTROL-click on the Mac) and choose Combine Slices from the drop-down menu. You will notice that slices 01 and 02 are now combined into one slice numbered slice 01. All the other numbers will update automatically.

5. Repeat steps 1 through 4 for slices 04 and 05.

Figure 4–12: Cleaned-up slices.

A. The side-navigation page sliced into zones.　B. The top-navigation page sliced into zones.

Figure 4-12 shows the side-navigation and top-navigation pages with the slices cleaned up. One slice now appears for each zone in each page: header, navigation, content, and footer.

THE WEB CONTENT PALETTE

The Web Content palette (choose Window | Web Content) is a great way to view and organize all your slices, tables, image maps, rollovers, and animations in Photoshop or ImageReady. As you create a feature, such as a slice, it will be automatically added to the palette. Figure 4-13 shows the slices in the Web Content palette.

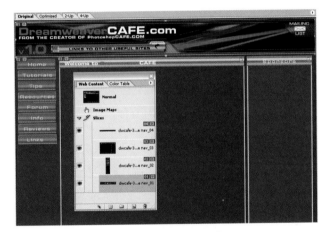

To display animations, click the options arrow at the upper right of the palette and choose Palette Options. Check the first option, Include Animation Frames, to

Figure 4–13: Slices in the Web Content palette.

show animation frames in the Web Content palette, or leave it unchecked to hide the frames. (They can still be viewed through the Animation palette.) Note that animations need to appear only if you are creating an animated rollover.

USING TABLES TO ORGANIZE SLICES

As you work with using sliced layouts in tables (in Dreamweaver at a later stage of your design), you'll begin to notice one drawback: when you move one slice, the entire table reshuffles (kind of like two people trying to sit on a beanbag chair).

This is a common problem that web designers experienced with earlier versions of ImageReady.

The solution to this problem is to use a *nested table*—a table inside a table. A nested table is a very efficient way to organize your content because you can manage the zones easily. Imagine that you created a separate table for each zone. Each table would contain the slices for its own zone, and, for example, the slices for the content and the navigation areas would be in separate tables. So when you make changes to the content table, the navigation table and zones would be totally unaffected. This is what using nested tables can help you do.

Converting Slices to Tables

ImageReady CS has a welcome new feature not found in previous versions: you can now define slices as tables. This allows you to break up the page into several smaller tables nested inside a master table. These smaller tables are easier to organize and update than one big table. In this section, you will arrange each zone into its own table. Then you will slice the image inside each table.

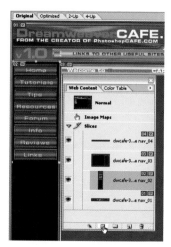

Let's convert the slices to tables:

1. Choose the first slice to convert to a table. In this case, select the slice that defines the navigation zone (slice 2).

2. At the bottom of the Web Content palette, click the Group Slice Into Table button, as shown in Figure 4–14.

In the Web Content palette, you will see that a new table has been created. The organization

Figure 4–14: Converting a slice to a table in the side-navigation layout.

works just like a layers set in the Layers palette. You can drag slices in and out of the table from and to the Web Content palette to add or remove them. Figure 4-15 shows the new table with a single nested slice.

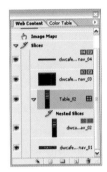

Figure 4–15: Organizing tables in the Web Content palette.

> **WARNING**
>
> When adjusting adjacent slices, be careful that they are in a rectangular block and aligned perfectly, or "extra" auto slices will be created.

3. Repeat these steps for each of the zones, until each zone is in its own table.

Figure 4-16 shows the page with each of the zones now defined as tables. The next step is to slice up all the images inside each table. This is a much more efficient way of slicing than just using slices on their own without tables. The page would still work without the nested tables, but a little extra effort now will save time in the long run. These nested tables will make it easier to separate the zones and update the web page in the future.

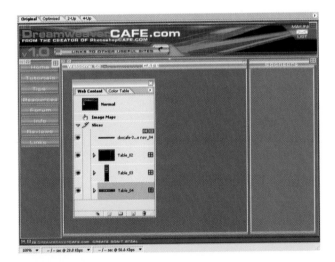

Figure 4–16: A page arranged into tables.

Manual Slicing

Now that the image is divided into tables, it's time to prepare the individual slices inside each zone. It's a good idea to prepare larger areas first and then move on to the smaller slices later. This way, you can arrange them more accurately. Remember that you want to get the job done cleanly and try to eliminate unnecessary slices.

> **TIP**
>
> Turn on the snap-to guides and snap-to slices in Photoshop and ImageReady. This will assist you in creating clean, accurate slices. You can find these options under View | Snap To, in the main menu.

Let's start with the header zone. We will begin with manual slicing:

1. Choose the Slice tool.

2. Click and drag to define a slice in the same way you would make a selection with the Marquee tool. In this example, I started at the top left and dragged over the header "Dreamweaver Café."

3. The slice (slice 01) will now appear and new auto slices will be created.

4. Click at the top left of the new slice and drag across the page for the next slice (slice 02).

5. Continue slicing: Figure 4–17 shows the sliced header zone divided into five slices.

Figure 4–17: Sliced header zone.

Figure 4-18 shows the Web Content palette after slicing the header. Notice that all the slices are nested under the table. You can click the little arrow to show/hide all the slices within a table.

Figure 4–18: Nested slices.

AVOIDING STRAY SLICES

Be on the lookout for slices that don't quite extend to the edges of the zone. Sometimes a slice is slightly off edge and this will create an additional slice that is difficult to track. Look to the slice numbering as a clue: Count the slices, and if the numbering suddenly jumps, you know an extra slice exists there somewhere. For example, Figure 4-19 shows a slice on the top that says 02 when you would expect it to be 01. Use the Slice Select tool to click and drag the edges to make adjustments.

Figure 4–19: Adjusting a slice.

Figure 4-20 shows the slice after the adjustment; notice it is now numbered 01. This clean slice will produce predictable results.

Figure 4–20: Clean slices.

> **TIP**
>
> While using the Slice tool, you can temporarily switch to the Slice Select tool by holding down the CTRL key (CMD on the Mac).

Slicing the Navigation—Creating Layer-Based Slices

In ImageReady, a layer-based slice is created when you choose a layer and convert its borders into a slice. Of course, all slices are rectangular in shape, so a layer that contains a circle will have a square-boundaried slice. Layer-based slices are quick to create and will cut an image as close to its edges as possible. This makes layer-based slices ideal for creating features such as buttons. As far as this project goes, you can create layer-based slices or create slices manually—it's up to you. But this technique can be handy to know, so read on.

To create a layer-based slice:

1. In the Layers palette, select the layer that will be sliced. Choose one of the navigation buttons on the web page.

2. Move the mouse cursor over the layer name and right-click (CONTROL-click on the Mac).

3. In the drop-down menu that opens, choose New Layer Based Slice, as shown in Figure 4-21.

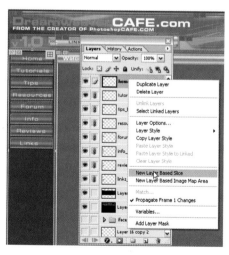

Figure 4–21: Creating a new layer-based slice.

4. A slice will appear around the layer. Repeat for each of the navigation buttons. Figure 4-22 shows the side-navigation area consisting of layer-based slices.

Figure 4-22: Layer-based slices.

A. Side navigation.   B. Top navigation.

Layer-based slices are ideal for navigation. They're quick to create, they create the smallest possible area for fast downloading, and they are flexible—if you move the layers, the slices will move with them, as shown in Figure 4-23.

However, layer-based slices should be avoided in content zones, because they create a lot of messy extra auto slices.

CONVERT MULTIPLE SLICES INTO A TABLE

When you created user slices, your slices stayed in the assigned tables. This is not the case with layer-based slices, however. The layer-based slices have been moved outside the table, but you can fix this by quickly arranging a region of slices into a table:

1. Open the Web Content palette.

Figure 4-23: Layer-based slices move with the layers.

2. Choose the first slice you want to add (choose any of the buttons).

3. Hold down the SHIFT key and click additional slices until all the desired slices are selected, as shown in Figure 4-24.

4. Click the Group Slice Into Table button.

Figure 4–24:
Selected slices.

As you can see in Figure 4-25, the navigation buttons are now grouped into a nested table. This will help keep them together if you want to modify the site later on.

At this point, you can continue slicing the entire page using the lessons you have learned so far in the chapter.

Figure 4–25: Nested tables.

TIP

You can add slices to a table by dragging them onto the table's name in the Web Content palette. You can remove slices by dragging them out of the table set.

SLICE SETS

A new tool, *sliced sets*, is available in ImageReady CS. Sliced sets allows you to slice an image in different ways and switch back and forth between the different slice sets. This is useful if you are mocking up a couple of ideas and want to present them on the Web—perhaps to show a client more than one option. Rather than save two different documents, you can save a layer comp and a slice set. Figure 4-26 shows a splash page with two different options. Obviously, the way the page is sliced works for the first idea, but it doesn't work for the second.

Figure 4–26: The mock up.

A. *The slices work.*   B. *The slices no longer work.*

If you take a look at the Web Content palette, you'll see three slices. Let's create a slice set:

1. Choose the New Slice Set button.

2. Drag the slices into the slice set, as shown in Figure 4-27. This set can now be hidden or shown by clicking the visibility icon.

3. Choose one of the slices that doesn't change between the two comps.

4. Click the New Slice Set button again to create a second slice set.

Figure 4–27: Moving slices into the set.

5. Hide the first set, as shown in Figure 4-28.

6. Show the different layer comp.

7. Create new slices for the second comp.

Notice in Figure 4-29 that as you show the different layer comps, you can now display a slice set to match each comp.

Figure 4–28: Hiding the first slice set.

Figure 4–29: The different slice sets.

Renaming Slices

By default, the slices are assigned a name based on a combination of the name of the document and its slice number. For example, if the document was called webpage.psd, the slice names would be webpage_01, webpage_02, and so on. As you can see, the names are probably not going to be useful if you try to make changes to the page at a later date. You can assign custom names to the slices that will override the auto names to make them recognizable later.

1. Select a slice with the Slice Select tool.
2. Open the Slice palette.
3. Under the Name field, enter a new name, such as *header* or *btn_home* (for a button labeled Home).

> **TIP**
>
> I suggest that you rename your slices with meaningful names; this will help you identify the images in the future.

CREATING IMAGE MAPS

Apart from slices, you can use other ways to define parts of images as clickable regions—for example, you may not want to slice an image exactly where you want it to be clickable, or it may have an irregular shape that doesn't lend itself well to sliced rectangles. An image map works by defining the coordinates of an image. When the mouse enters those coordinates, it is detected, and when the user clicks, he or she jumps to a new link—*usually*. An image map comes in two flavors: server side (SS) and client side (CS). A server-side image map uses server technology to define the region, whereas a client-side image map calculations are made on the user's machine. Server software is necessary for the former, but ImageReady creates the latter, so special server software is not necessary to set it up.

Figure 4–30 shows my working web page that contains a Mailing List button at the top right. The slice is a bit too big to accommodate the button, so let's create an image map to trigger the link to the mailing list.

1. In ImageReady, choose the Image Map tool from the Tool palette, as shown in Figure 4-30. You'll see three options:

   • **Rectangular Image:** Map Tool Creates rectangular-shaped image maps

   • **Circle Image Map Tool:** Creates circular- and elliptical-shaped image maps

   • **Polygon Image Map Tool:** Creates irregular-shaped image maps

Figure 4–30: Choosing the Image Map tool.

2. Choose the Polygon tool to create an irregular-shaped map.

3. To define the region, click around the shape; a line will be drawn to connect the clicks.

4. Continue until you have completed and closed the path.

5. The image map is now created, indicating which area will respond to a mouse click. Now let's decide where we should be directed when we click the image map. Open the Image Map palette from the Window Menu.

6. In the URL field, type in the name of the link. If the targeted page is in a directory on the same server (internal), type in its name, such as info.htm—this is called a *relative* link. If the user is to be directed

to a page on another server (external), type in an absolute link, such as **http://www.dreamweavercafe.com**. Figure 4-31 shows a relative link entered.

That's all you need to do. When the page is exported (see Chapter 5 for more information), ImageReady will do all the difficult stuff, like coding, for you.

Figure 4–31: Defining the link.

CREATING A ROLLOVER EFFECT

A *rollover* is one of the easiest ways to add interactivity to your web page. Rollovers have become tremendously popular in web design. A rollover is a great way to make a button tempting to click. Nowadays, rollovers can be created with ease because of programs such as ImageReady; they are almost a standard feature of interactivity. Users are beginning to expect rollovers on all web sites they visit. When the user hovers his or her mouse over a button, it changes—perhaps the button glows or changes color. This indicates that something will happen if the button is clicked.

A rollover is simply an image (usually a slice) that changes when it detects the presence of the mouse. You simply swap out one image for another of the same size to create the rollover. These different images are called *states*. Typically, only the *normal* and *over* states are used because the file size associated with a new image for each state is usually pretty large. Here are the states available:

- **Normal State:** How the button looks in its default state

- **Over State:** How the button looks when a mouse moves over the area

- **Down State:** How the button looks as a mouse button is clicked

- **Selected:** How the button remains changed after a mouse button has been clicked

- **Out:** How the button changes when a mouse moves out of the area

- **Up:** How the button changes when the mouse button is released

- **Click:** How the button remains changed after the mouse has been clicked, until the mouse moves outside the area

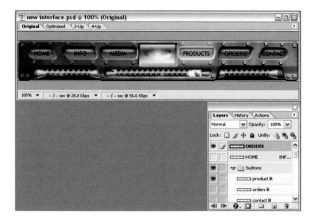

Figure 4–32A shows how a rollover effect is achieved in the Layers palette. Notice that as the product lit layer is shown, it appears as if the button is glowing. This effect is created using layers. A rollover can also be as simple as attaching a layer effect and hiding the effect until the mouse rolls over the area, as we will add to our project and as shown in Figure 4-32B. Figure 4-33 shows a standard Inner Shadow blending option and a

Figure 4–32A: Changing the layer to give the appearance of a button changing.

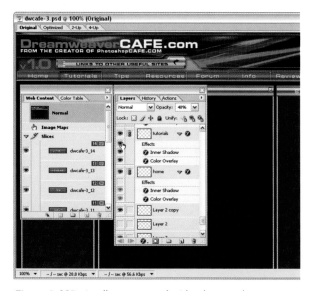

Figure 4–32B: A rollover created with a layer style.

custom Color Overlay layer style. You should, of course, create the effects that best suit your page. (See Chapter 3 for more on layer styles.)

Now that you know that you can create the illusion of a button changing by hiding and showing layers or effects, you need to find a way to detect the mouse and have this happen automatically. This is very easy to achieve in ImageReady:

Figure 4–33: The layer style used to create the rollover effect.

Figure 4–34: Selecting the slice.

1. Choose the slice to which you want to apply the rollover effect. As you select the slice, it will be highlighted in the Web Content palette, as shown in Figure 4–34. Let's begin with the Home button. You can also select your slice right here in the Web Control palette simply by clicking it.

2. Click the Create Rollover State button in the Web Content palette (at the bottom of Figure 4–35).

3. A new state will be created, called *Over*. This state will appear when a mouse rolls over the area. By default, the new state will be selected, as shown in Figure 4–35.

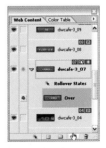

Figure 4–35: Creating a new Over state.

4. To complete the rollover effect, make a change in the Layers palette. In this case, show the layer style by clicking the eye icon next to the word *Effects*, as shown at right in Figure 4-36.

Figure 4-36: Changing the layers to create the rollover effect.

5. Once the effect has been created, it's a good idea to click back on the normal state, as shown in Figure 4-37, to avoid changing anything by accident. Notice as you click the normal state that the effect is turned off again. You can see the effect in the Over thumbnail.

6. Repeat these steps for all the buttons on your page.

Figure 4-37: Returning to the normal state.

7. You can preview your rollover by choosing the preview button from the Tool palette (the button next to it will launch the web browser and let you preview the entire page).

Remote Rollovers

A remote rollover (sometimes called a *disjointed* rollover) occurs when more than one slice is affected by the rollover activity. This is great to use for menus. For example, as you roll your mouse over a button, it will simultaneously change another portion of the image, which will display some information, such as the contents of the link you are about to click. You can see examples of this at **www.dreamweavercafe.com** or **www.photoshopcafe.com**.

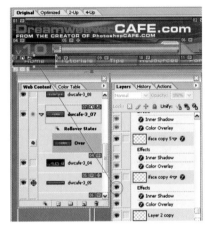

Figure 4–38: Using layer effects for a rollover state.

1. Create the rollover in the normal manner. Figure 4-38 shows an example of using layer effects to create a recessed look to the button.

2. With the Over state selected, make the additional changes to the layer of the remote slice. In this case, add the text "Back to the Homepage" on slice 05.

3. Finally, let ImageReady know that you want to use slice 05 as the remote slice by targeting it. To target a slice, use the little squiggly shape next to the Over state in the Web Content palette. Click and drag the mouse from the squiggly into the target slice, as shown in Figure 4-39.

Figure 4–39: Targeting a remote slice.

When you test the page in a web browser, as shown in Figure 4-40, the remote text should change as you move our mouse over the button. You can see this in action at **www.dreamweavercafe.com**.

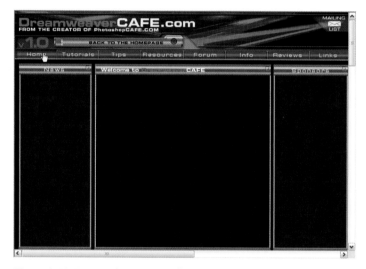

Figure 4–40: Testing the remote rollover.

Adding Hyperlinks to the Buttons

Whether or not you have created rollovers for your buttons, they will do nothing when you click them unless you define a hyperlink. Let's now attach links to each of our buttons.

1. Open the page in ImageReady if it isn't already open.

2. Open the Slice palette.

3. With the Slice Select tool, click a navigation button.

4. Type the link into the URL field, as shown in Figure 4-41. (The Target field determines in which window the link will open. Leave these blank for the site. Hyperlinks are covered in detail in Chapter 7.)

Figure 4–41: Creating a hyperlink.

TIP

You can create alt text in the Slice palette for any slice on the page. This will display the text you add in place of the image before it has loaded. Alt text helps with accessibility for viewers who have disabilities by allowing a page reader to identify the image.

Attach links to the remainder of the buttons. I have used index.htm, tutorials.htm, tips.htm, resources.htm, forum.htm, info.htm, reviews.htm, and links.htm. We will create pages for each of these links with the same names in Chapter 8.

In the next chapter, you are going to learn about image optimization, and you'll publish your first page as HTML.

CHAPTER 5

THE NEED FOR SPEED: MAKING THE PAGE LOAD QUICKLY AND EFFICIENTLY

This chapter examines various image formats and compression. You will learn which format is best for your particular needs. After exploring file-optimization methods and applying a workflow to a web project, you will learn how to export a page for viewing on the Internet. This is the final chapter in the Photoshop/ImageReady workflow; your web page will be ready to open in Dreamweaver by the end of this chapter.

WHY OPTIMIZE?

When you optimize an image for inclusion on a web page, your goal is to reduce the file size of the image to make it load faster on a viewer's machine. Because a smaller file size will result in faster loading pages, this becomes a very important subject. No matter how great your pages look, if they take forever to load, people will become impatient and click to another site.

Although the popularity of high-speed Internet—such as DSL (digital subscriber line), T1, and cable broadband services—means that load time isn't as much of an issue for many web users as it used to be with dial-up access, remember that not everyone has broadband. It is also not as popular in most countries outside the United States because of the high cost of such service. So it's not a good idea to think that the widespread use of broadband means you don't have to optimize.

Optimizing images is a balancing act. On one hand, you want to produce the smallest possible file size; on the other hand, you want to use the best-looking image possible. While optimizing, you may discover a trade-off between quality and file size. However, a well-optimized page will lose practically no quality and will still load quickly.

MEASURING IMAGE SIZE AND SPEED

To measure the size and speed of your graphics, consider the following:

- **The image size:** Measured in kilobytes (K or KB): 1024 bytes=1 kilo-byte; 1024 kilobytes=1 megabyte (MB).

- **The speed of the connection:** Typical dial-up modems transfer at 56 Kbps (kilobits per second), although in reality a 56 Kbps modem will rarely establish a connection faster than 33 Kbps. A DSL will connect at anywhere from 256 to 720 Kbps, and cable modems can typically run at 1.5 Mbps (megabits per second). One byte=8 bits and 1 kilo-byte=8192 bits.

To see how long an 8K image would take to download on a 56 Kbps modem, we would have to first convert 8K into kilobits: 65.5 (8x8.192=65,536). At 56 Kbps, you can see it would take just over 1 second for the 65.5 kilobit image to download.

The Easy Way to Calculate Download Times

Fortunately, you can use an easier and faster way to tell how long your images will take to download. ImageReady does all the calculations for you and displays the information in the Status Bar. Click the Optimize tab at the top of the image, and then choose the speed of the connection from a menu at the bottom of the Status Bar, as shown in Figure 5-1.

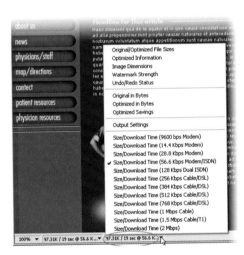

Figure 5–1: The download time for this preoptimized web page is 19 seconds on a 56.6 Kbps modem.

VIEWING OPTIMIZED IMAGES

When you launch ImageReady, you will notice the four tabs across the top of the document window. The Original tab shows the "live" image in its uncompressed state, and this is where you will perform all your work. The Optimized tab shows how the image would look if it were exported with the current optimization settings. The 2-Up tab allows you to compare the original image and the optimized image, as shown in Figure 5-2. Notice that all the file specs are displayed under the images. As you change the optimization settings, the Optimized window will update in real time.

Figure 5–2: Comparing the original and optimized images.

The 4–Up tab allows you to compare the result of different optimization settings. To select a pane, click it, and it will shows the settings that will be applied to the image when you choose Save | Optimized.

> **NOTE**
>
> These tabs also appear in Photoshop's Save For Web feature, accessed by choosing File | Save For Web.

CHOOSING THE CORRECT WAY TO COMPRESS YOUR IMAGES

To make your images load faster during optimization, you must *compress* them and save them in various formats, as discussed next. These file formats compress images in different ways. Knowing how a file is compressed and the advantages and dis-advantages of each type of compression will help you choose the best way to com-press your images.

GIF (Graphics Interchange Format)

GIF is the best file format to use for solid colors, patterns, or vector-style images such as cartoons. This format works well with text and can work for photographs, although it's not the first choice for photos because it can display only a maximum of 256 colors. The GIF format reduces the file size mainly by reducing the num-ber of colors in an image. The GIF format will also scan the image for repeating patterns of pixels and index these to reduce the file size even further.

To optimize an image as a GIF:

1. In ImageReady, choose the Optimize, 2-Up, or 4-Up tab.

2. Open the Optimize palette.

3. Choose GIF as the format.

4. In the Reduction field, choose an algorithm:

- **Perceptual:** Gives preference to colors that are predominantly vis-ible to the human eye

- **Selective:** Produces the most accurate color table (default works best for most purposes)

- **Adaptive:** Uses the most common colors in the image

- **Restrictive Web:** Uses the 216 web-safe colors (see the Web-Safe Colors section in Chapter 2)

5. In the Colors field, indicate the number of colors you want the image to reduce to, as shown in Figure 5-3A. Open the Color Table palette to see the colors that are used in the image, as shown in Figure 5-3B. You can choose one of the following options:

- Choose the number of colors from the drop-down menu and let ImageReady decide the colors to keep (calculated by your chosen algorithm), as shown in Figure 5-3A.

- Select the colors in the Color Table and click the trash can icon to dispose of the colors manually (Figure 5-3B). You will also notice a button that looks like a cube in this palette. This is the Color Shift button; clicking it will shift the color to the closest web-safe color. You can use this option to protect against dithering in older computers running 256 colors. (See Chapter 2 for more on web-safe colors.)

Figure 5-3: Reducing the colors.

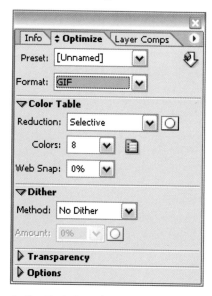

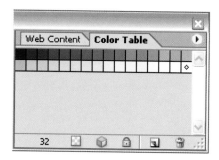

A. The Optimize palette.   B. The Color Table.

6. To find the best optimization setting, experiment with different ones until you find a solution that looks OK and has a reasonable file size. I usually slowly reduce the image until it begins to look bad and then tweak it up just a little. Figure 5-4 shows an original image (top left) compared to GIFs set at 256, 64, and 8 colors. Notice how the text and solid color look good even a low settings and the photographic portion shows banding (harsh transitions in the gradients) with the GIF format.

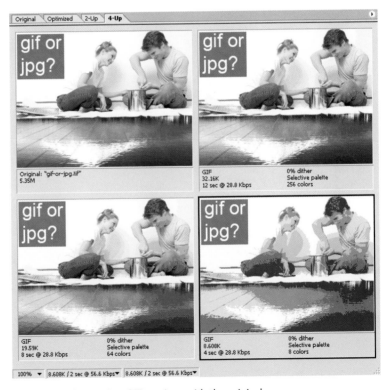

Figure 5–4: Comparing GIF settings with the original.

Dithering

The last important setting on the Optimize palette for GIFs is the Dither setting. As discussed in Chapter 2, dithering occurs when tiny dots are added to an image in an attempt to smoothen out harsh transitions. In some cases, dithering can improve the appearance of the image, but it will increase the file size. As a rule of thumb, dither an image only if you are using limited colors and the image looks bad without it. Figure 5-5 shows a 16-color image dithered (left) and undithered (right); notice how dithering smoothes out the photo but increases the file size.

Figure 5–5: Dithering an image.

> **NOTE**
>
> When you save an image as a GIF, it will be converted to *indexed color mode* (choose Image | Mode) because it is using a reduced color palette.

Two more features of GIF make the format a viable choice. GIF supports 1-bit transparency, which allows you to create images that appear to be shapes other than rectangles. All images are created as rectangles, but in GIF, the image will appear transparent except where pixels are present. This transparency is limited—either it's on or off—and you cannot create smooth transitions or semi-transparent sections. GIF also supports animation. (Both transparency and animation are covered in Chapter 9.)

JPEG (Joint Photographic Experts Group)

The JPG (pronounced "jay-peg") file format is best for photographs and images than contain soft shadows or gradients. JPG compresses images by discarding image detail. This is known as a *lossy* format, because the image loses quality as more compression is applied. On higher settings, you would not notice the difference between the original and the compressed image. This type of compression is very efficient, and you can use it to reduce the file size of an image substantially.

Open the Optimize palette in ImageReady and choose the JPEG format. You will notice an option called Quality. Click the amount slider and choose a setting between 0 and 100, as shown in Figure 5-6.

Lower Quality settings will produce the smallest file sizes but also the lowest quality images. Higher settings will produce sharp-looking images, but the file size increases the

Figure 5–6: Optimizing a JPEG image.

higher you go. The challenge is to choose the smallest file size that still looks acceptable. Figure 5-7 shows an image with different amounts of compression applied; notice on the highly compressed image that a few *artifacts* (the unsightly textures introduced to smooth areas of the image) appear, especially in the areas of solid color.

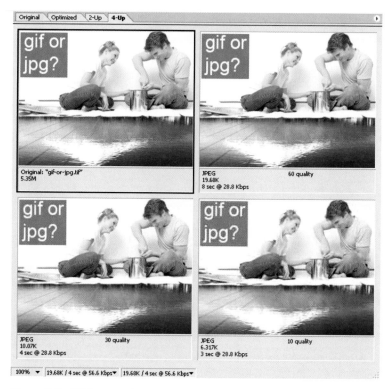

Figure 5–7: JPEG comparison.

Under Quality in the Optimize palette, you'll see a Blur option. A blurred image will compress better than a sharp image in the JPG format. If you need to squeeze a little extra out of your image, add a small amount of blur; this can also help if a lot of artifacts appear on your image.

> **TIP**
>
> The best JPG Optimization setting for use on the Web is between 30 and 50.

Click the Options arrow and you will see an option called Progressive. A progressive JPG image will load in several passes. A low-quality image (called a *proxy*) will load very quickly; this will give the viewer something to look at immediately. After the proxy has loaded, the image will increase in quality as its details continue to load.

NOTE

Unlike GIF, JPEG does not support transparency or animation.

PNG (Portable Network Graphics)

A third type of file type is the PNG (pronounced "ping"). PNG is not as popular as JPG or GIF, because not all browsers support this format. But PNG has a lot of potential, and with increased support we will see more of this format used in the future. PNG images come in two flavors:

- **PNG-8:** This works much like a GIF except that no animation support is available. A PNG-8 produces a smaller size file than a GIF and is a valid alternative for nongradient images.

- **PNG-24:** This *lossless* format preserves a quality image. PNG-24 is unique in that it supports *alpha channels*, which means that you can produce an image with 256 levels of transparencies and that semi-opaque and soft shadows are possible. The disadvantage: apart from lack of browser support, the file sizes are larger than JPG, so use this format only when it's essential to create 8-bit transparency (256 levels). No user controls are available for the settings of this format, compression is automatic, and no animation support is available. PNG-24 is the favored format for exporting images with transparency to Macromedia Flash.

SWF (Macromedia Flash)

New in ImageReady CS is the ability to export to SWF (pronounced "swiff"), the native output for Flash. The advantage of this format is that it is vector-based; this means that all shape layers and text will remain as vectors, resulting in very small file sizes and sharp images. SWF handles animation better than any other format. Its only drawback is that the viewer will need to have the Flash plug-in installed on his or her computer to view the files.

OPTIMIZING SLICED IMAGES

Now let's pick up our project and apply what you have just learned to our work-in-progress web page. Here's how you apply these settings in a practical workflow.

Selecting Multiple Slices

A quick way to start optimizing images is to perform a "wholesale optimization"—that is, perform a general optimization over the whole page and then fine-tune individual slices (see Chapter 4) that require special attention.

1. Select more than one slice at a time by one of two methods:
   - Click with the Slice Select tool to select the first slice. Hold down the SHIFT key and click additional slices to add them to the selection. SHIFT-click a selected slice to remove it from the selection.
   - Click and drag with the Slice Select tool to select a block of slices.

2. Choose the Optimized tab at the top of the page so that you can view the results of the settings.

3. Select all the slices in the header and navigation areas of your page, as shown in Figure 5–8.

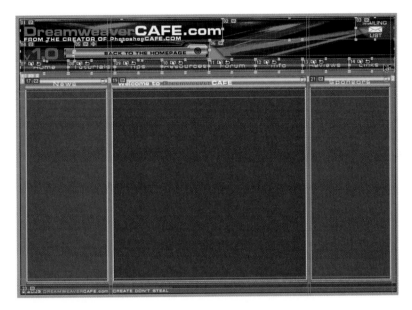

Figure 5–8: Selecting multiple slices.

4. Because this area contains mainly images and gradients, choose a JPG Quality Amount setting of 42, as shown in Figure 5-9. (Note that if a header is mainly flat color, you would choose GIF in this step.)

Figure 5–9: Choosing optimization settings.

5. Repeat steps 1 through 4 for the content portion of the page. Select all the slices and choose GIF for the format, as shown in Figure 5-10. Choose a setting that retains the look of the page with the minimum possible colors. I have chosen a setting of 16 colors for this design.

Figure 5–10: Optimizing GIFs.

View the page, and you'll probably notice that the navigation buttons are not looking good as JPEGs. Artifacts appear and the text is distorted, making it difficult to read. Text often looks best when compressed as a GIF image.

6. Select all the button slices.

7. Choose GIF for the format and push the Color setting up to 128 colors, as shown in Figure 5-11.

TIP

It's usually a good idea to make navigation buttons as sharp as possible; this is one place you don't want to skip on quality.

Figure 5–11: Setting the buttons as GIFs.

Fine-Tuning the Optimization Settings

Now it's time to hone in on the individual slices and work toward the best possible optimized settings. Look for slices that are suffering from degradation, such as slices with text. We will experiment to see whether JPEG or GIF formats will work better for individual slices.

Set up the page so that you can view the results of the optimization—not just those in quality but those in the file size of the individual slices. Choose a setting that will enable you to view the file size of the selected slice.

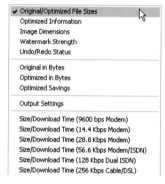

Figure 5-12: Choosing a setting that will enable you to view the size of a slice.

1. At the bottom of the document palette, click the arrow on the Status Bar and select Original/Optimized File Sizes, as shown in Figure 5-12.

The text on the banner is blurry because of the high JPG compression. We could use a higher JPG setting or change the format to GIF. Let's find out which works best.

2. Increase the Quality of the slice until the text looks sharp. An Amount setting of 77 is high enough. The size of the slice is 17.15K, as we can see in the Status bar in Figure 5-13.

Figure 5-13: Viewing the file size of the JPEG at a 77 Quality setting.

3. Now compare the size to a GIF. Choose GIF for the Format an dchoose the lowest setting that looks good. In Figure 5-14, 128 col-

ors was chosen. Notice that the file size is 12.28K. This is a 5K savings over the JPG format, and it looks as good, so it looks like the GIF is the winner in this case.

4. Continue optimizing each slice. Notice that the JPG shows artifacts in the display in Figure 5-15.

5. Change the Format to GIF and notice how much better this slice looks in Figure 5-16. In this instance, GIF works better; test your own page and use the format that works best for the image you are using. Usually, slices with text look better as GIFs, but that isn't always the case. If the area around the text contains photos or gradients, a higher JPG setting may work better. Choose the best-looking option with the lowest file size.

Work over the rest of your page and finish optimizing each slice. When you are done, it's time to think about the next step: adding hyperlinks.

Figure 5–14: Choosing a GIF and comparing its file size.

Figure 5–15: Artifacts caused by JPG.

Figure 5–16: The slice changed to a GIF.

PREVIEWING IN THE BROWSER

Preview the page in a browser to make sure that the adjacent slices match when you mix file formats. In some cases, a GIF can cause a color shift. If that happens, it's best to reoptimize or keep the adjacent slices in the same format, even if the file size is a little larger that way.

Figure 5–17: The browser's Preview button.

To preview in the browser, click the Preview button shown in Figure 5-17 (in this case, it's the Internet Explorer icon).

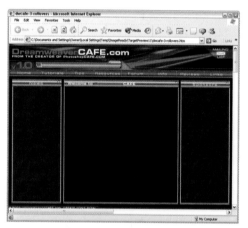

The page will launch in your web browser, as shown in Figure 5-18. Check the images carefully to make sure that the optimization looks good. At this point, you should also test your rollovers and make sure they function correctly.

Figure 5–18: Previewing the image in the browser.

ADDING HYPERLINKS

Hyperlinks are the "hot links" on a web site that people click to get around on the Web. Each button should have a hyperlink attached to it that will take the visitor to another page (either on the same site or somewhere on the Web). You assign these links in the URL (Uniform Resource Locator) field in the Slice palette. Here's how it's done:

1. Open the Slice palette.

2. Choose the Slice Select tool and click the first (Home) button.

3. In the URL field, add the link to which you want the hyperlink to go. For the home button in Figure 5-19, I chose index.htm.

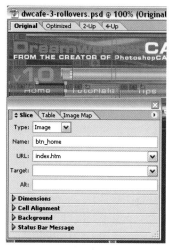

Figure 5–19: Assigning a URL.

4. Add a hyperlink for each navigation button. On the Dreamweaver-CAFE site, I choose Tutorials.htm, Tips.htm, and so on, to coincide with the labels on the buttons. When choosing names that describe your pages, try to keep them short and don't include spaces. Although

links will work with spaces in the names, it could cause problems with some UNIX web servers, so it's best to avoid them. A common practice is to substitute an underscore for a space, like so: *the_space*. Also, try to use the same case in the name; lowercase is the accepted format.

5. To create image maps, choose the Image Map palette from the Window menu if it's not visible in the main window.

6. Fill out the URL field just as you would in the Slices palette.

Now is an excellent time to save you work if haven't already done so. (After being the victim of too many computer crashes and power outages, I now save whenever I change anything.)

ADDING E-MAIL LINKS

To assign a hyperlink, you add the name of the URL. You can also add an e-mail address: use the mailto:*youraddress@whatever.com* tag. When you type **mailto:**, the web browser launches the e-mail program on your computer and enters the address into the To: field. Figure 5-20 shows an e-mail address typed into the URL field.

Figure 5–20: Adding an e-mail link.

> **TIP**
>
> If you want the subject line to be filled out automatically in the e-mail, add the ?subject="*subject name*" tag at the end of the address. Here's how it might look: mailto:webmaster@dreamweavercafe.com?subject="about the book"

EXPORTING

After you have optimized the page and set up all the hyperlinks, it's time to export everything into HTML. It's a very simple task to take the page that you have created in ImageReady and make it an HTML page:

Figure 5–21: Choosing a location to export the new site.

1. Choose File | Save Optimized As.

2. Select a destination on your computer's hard drive.

3. Create a new folder—in the case of Figure 5-21, I named it *site*.

4. Choose a file name; I named the file *dwcafe.html*.

5. Click OK, and everything will be exported to the folder.

6. If you open the folder you created, you will notice two files, similar to those shown in Figure 5-22. One is the HTML document and the other is an image folder. Double-click the HTML document and the web page will launch in your web browser. (On the Mac, you may also drag the file to your browser window to launch it.)

Figure 5–22:
The new web files.

7. Open the images folder and you will see all the image slices you saved, as shown in Figure 5-23.

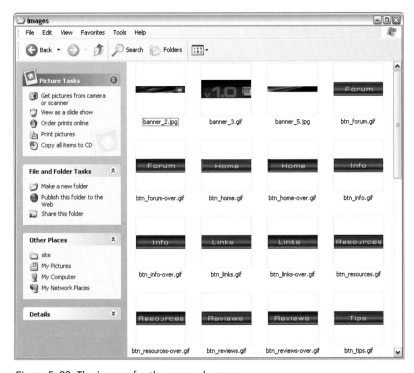

Figure 5–23: The images for the new web page.

The HTML page is now ready for opening in Dreamweaver in the next chapter.

SAVE FOR WEB

If you are working in Photoshop and you want to export images for the Web, you can access most of the functionality of ImageReady from the Save For Web dialog box shown in Figure 5-24 (choose File | Save For Web). You cannot create advanced features such as rollovers or animations from here, but you can optimize images and export them.

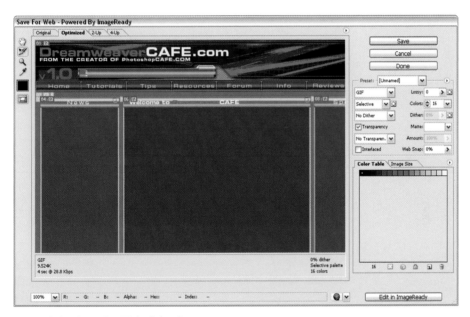

Figure 5–24: Save For Web dialog box.

PART III

WORK IN DREAMWEAVER

CHAPTER 6

BUILDING THE HOME PAGE

Whether you are creating an entirely new site completely in Dreamweaver or importing a layout from Photoshop/ImageReady, the initial process is the same. The first thing you need to do is set up Dreamweaver to recognize the files as a web site and to manage the assets effectively. This is called *defining* a site. When you define a site, you are selecting a location on your computer where all the files associated with this new site will be kept.

SETTING UP A NEW SITE IN DREAMWEAVER

When you launch Dreamweaver, you will see the welcome screen shown in Figure 6-1. From this screen, you can create new pages or open existing pages. To begin the process of defining a site, click the Dreamweaver site button (labeled Define A New Site in Figure 6-1).

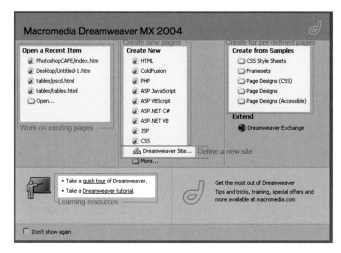

Figure 6–1: The welcome screen.

Alternatively, you can choose Site | Manage Sites and the Manage Sites dialog box will open, as shown in Figure 6-2. Here you can manage different web site definitions. Let's create a new site defini-tion: click the New button to start the def-inition process.

Figure 6–2: The Manage Sites dialog box.

You will see the Site Definition dialog box, where you enter all the information that pertains to the site. Notice the two tabs at the top—Basic and Advanced. If you are familiar with defining sites, the Advanced window will give you the most control, as you can simply enter the desired settings. Figure 6-3 shows the Advanced Site Definition window.

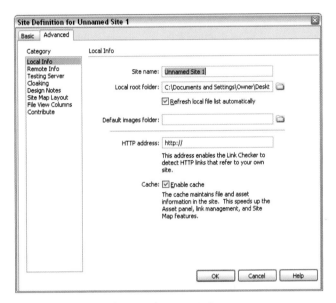

Figure 6–3: Advanced Site Definition window.

If this is all new to you, the best option is to choose the Basic tab, as shown in Figure 6-4.

Figure 6–4: Basic Site Definition window.

1. Enter the name of your new site.

2. Click the Next button to proceed to the next screen, shown in Figure 6-5, which will ask whether you want to use server technology, which is used for connecting to databases for dynamic sites. Click the No button; we will not be using databases on this site, as dynamic sites are beyond the scope of this book.

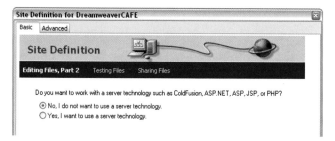

Figure 6–5: Server technology screen.

3. Click the Next button.

4. In the next screen, choose the location for the web site. You will see two radio buttons: keep the default option selected to edit on the local

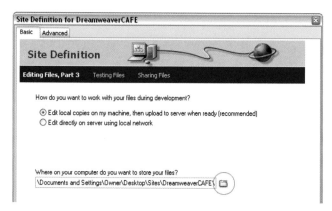

Figure 6–6: Choosing the location for your files.y screen.

computer. Click the folder button to choose the location for your site, as shown in Figure 6-6.

5. Navigate to the folder where you saved your site files. (We exported the site from ImageReady into this folder in Chapter 5.) Figure 6-7 shows the Site folder selected. Click Select and then Next.

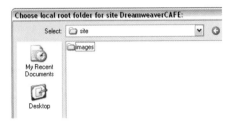

Figure 6–7: Choosing your site's location.

6. The next window is the Sharing Files window, shown in Figure 6-8. Here you set up the information to connect to the remote server (web server). You will not do this until Chapter 12, so choose None from the drop-down menu for now.

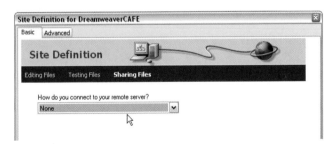

Figure 6–8: Defining the remote server.

7. Click the Next button and you will see a Summary page, as shown in Figure 6-9.

8. Click Done to finish the site definition.

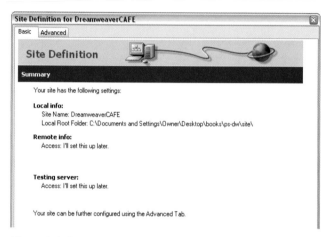

Figure 6–9: Summary page.

9. You will now see the Manage Sites dialog box, as shown in Figure 6-10, with your new site added to the list of sites. Click Done.

Figure 6–10: Your new site is now on the list.

OPENING A PAGE IN DREAMWEAVER

You have finished defining the site. If you look at the Files palette in Dreamweaver, you will see all the files that are currently in the folder. If the Files palette is not visible, choose it from the Window menu.

The Files palette is where you manage all the files in your site. Click the Expand button (circled in Figure 6-11) to expand this palette.

When the palette is expanded, as shown in Figure 6-12, you will see two windows. The window on the right shows all the files in the web folder on the local system.

The window on the left shows all the files on the web server; this is how you will navigate the remote server later on. (We will explore the remote file management and FTP features in Chapter 12, so don't be concerned about this right now.) Click the Expand button again to contract the window to the smaller palette.

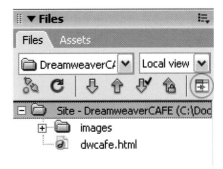

Figure 6–11: The Files palette.

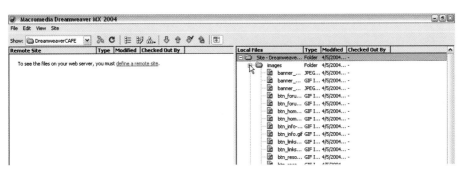

Figure 6–12: Expanded palette.

To launch a page in Dreamweaver, simply double-click the page's icon in the File palette, as shown in Figure 6–13. Double-click your exported web page now.

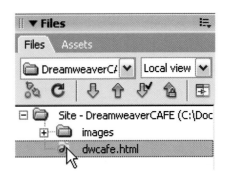

Figure 6–13: Launching a page from the Files palette.

USING THE DREAMWEAVER WORKSPACE

The Dreamweaver workspace can be divided into four main areas:

- **Document area:** Where you work on your documents. You view and work on the design layout and code in this window.

- **Insert bar:** Used to insert all kinds of elements onto the page. Choose the type of elements from a category on the drop-down menu.

- **Property Inspector:** A context-sensitive menu used to modify the settings of various elements.

- **Panels:** All the panels (called *palettes* in Photoshop) open in this region.

In the upper left, above the document area, are three view options: Code, Split, and Design. Design view is the default setting; this is the most visual setting and is shown in Figure 6-14. Click each of the buttons shown in Figure 6-14 to change views.

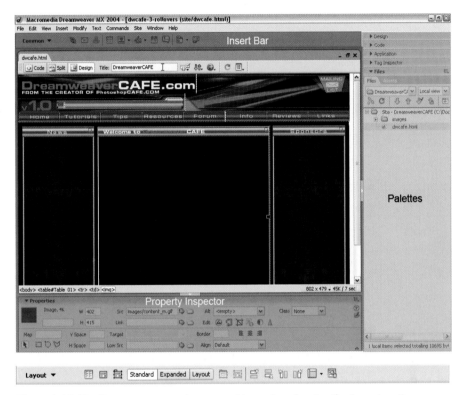

Figure 6–14: The Dreamweaver workspace and Insert bar showing the Layout option.

Figure 6-15 shows the Code view. When this option is enabled, the document area will show all the HTML code. If you are familiar with HTML, you could write all your code directly in this area and build your site this way. Many features are included to help you write code, including line numbers, word wrap, color coding, and drop-down code hints.

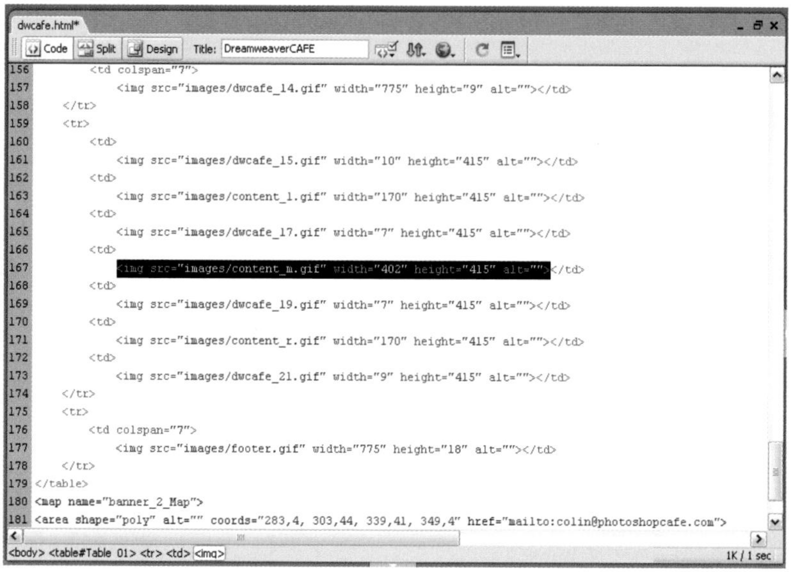

Figure 6–15: Code view.

A third option is the Split view, which displays a split window where you can see both the Design and the Code views at the same time. As you select an object in the Design view in the lower panel, the associated code is selected in the upper Code view panel, as shown in Figure 6-16. This is a great setup for making manual tweaks in the code. An added advantage of Split view is that you can use it to help you learn HTML.

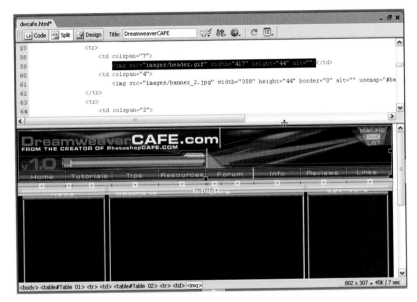

Figure 6–16: Split view.

Maximizing Your Screen Area

When designing, there never seems to be enough screen space. A useful feature can help you maximize your screen real estate. Notice a small bar with an arrow in between screen regions; this is called the Collapse button. Figure 6-17 shows the cursor hovered over this button.

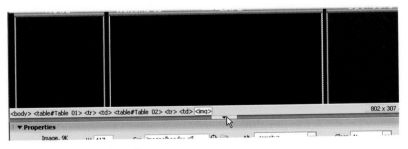

Figure 6–17: The Collapse button.

Click this button to expand and collapse panels in Dreamweaver. Figure 6–18 shows the Property Inspector collapsed. (This is possible in Windows only, because the Mac uses a floating-palette system.)

Figure 6–18: The collapsed Property Inspector.

Finding Help

To expand and collapse a panel, click the little arrow next to the panel header.

> **TIP**
>
> You can detach a panel from the group by clicking at the upper left of a panel and dragging it into the document area. You can then resize the panel to any size you choose.

Under the Code panel, you will see a Reference tab, a useful option that contains several code reference books from O'Reilly, Wrox, and Macromedia. Choose the type of reference from the drop-down menu. The Reference panel will display the information, as shown in Figure 6-19.

TIP

If the Reference panel is not available, press SHIFT-F1 to show it.

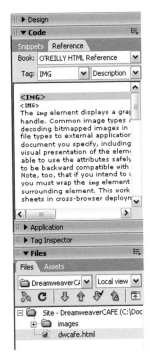

Figure 6–19:
Reference panel.

Ordering the Tables

In the Standard view, it can be difficult to see where the cells in the tables meet. If you click an image, it will be highlighted, allowing you to see the edges. Finding small slices and selecting empty cells used to be a real circus act. I say "used to" because with Dreamweaver MX 2004, a new feature called Expanded Tables mode adds space around each cell and shows the borders. This is an excellent feature, because it allows you to see the layout clearly and to select different cells easily. This mode does not reflect how a final page will appear; instead, it assists you in selecting cells and working with tables.

To show the Expanded Tables mode, choose Layout from the left side of the Insert bar. Then click the Expanded button, as shown in Figure 6–20.

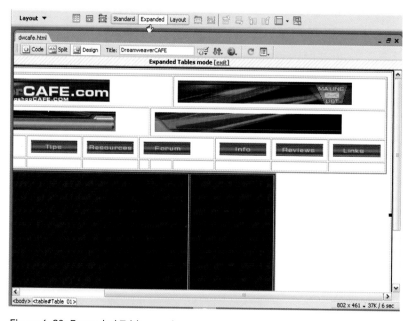

Figure 6–20: Expanded Tables mode.

TIP

If the Insert bar is not available, press CTRL/CMD-F2 to display it.

PREPARING THE CONTENT ZONE OF YOUR DESIGN

Now that we have had a quick tour of Dreamweaver's workspace, let's continue with the project. By now, you probably realize that you will be facing a challenge if you want to add text to your page. If you click the content zone, you'll see that images occupy the space. If you want to add text, you must remove these images and replace them with empty cells so that you can type your text and import other elements. You can use several techniques to maintain the appearance of the page, such as filling cells with color and using the images as background elements, allowing you to type in text. We will walk through some of these techniques in this section.

First, select the content zone and then delete everything. You can then create an empty table and use this as the "container" for the content of the web site.

> **NOTE**
>
> You could create CSS layers and place the text over the top of the existing lay-out. This is a quick solution, but it increases the file size, and if you change the alignment of the page, the positioning of the layers is difficult to maintain.

1. Open your working page in Dreamweaver if you haven't already done so.

2. Choose the Expanded Tables mode so that you can clearly see all the cells.

3. Click and hold inside the bottom-left cell that you want to select. (Be careful to select the cell and not its contents—if you selected the contents by accident, try reclicking.)

4. Hold and drag your mouse diagonally until all the cells you want to work with are selected, as shown in Figure 6-21. (If all the content is in a single cell, just select that cell.) You can also select the `<td>` tag on the bottom of the screen (the Tag Inspector) to select the cell's contents.

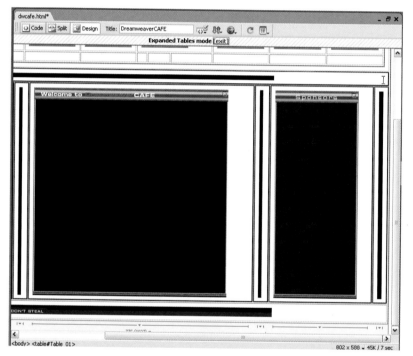

Figure 6–21: All the cells selected.

5. Press the DELETE key to delete everything from the content zone. An empty cell should result, as shown in Figure 6-22.

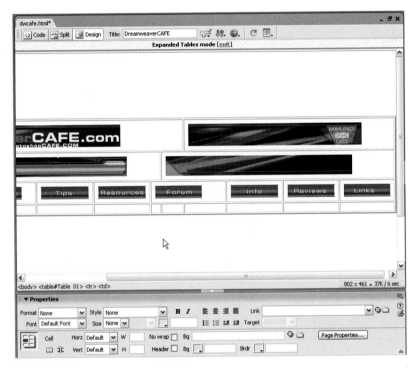

Figure 6–22: Deleting all the excess content.

We will now view the Standard Tables view.

6. Either click the Standard button from the Layout options or click the highlighted *[exit]* text above the layout window. Your layout should now be displayed with the navigation elements all together and an empty content area like that shown in Figure 6-23. If it doesn't work the way you expect, undo the operation (CTRL-Z) and try selecting and deleting again.

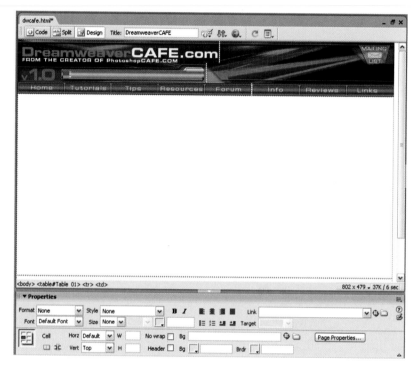

Figure 6–23: The page in Standard Tables view.

Creating a Nested Table

Now we'll create a new table that will act as a container for our content. You may remember that nested tables were discussed in Chapter 4—a nested table is a table within a table. Nested tables are a great way to control the layout and organize content.

1. Click the cell inside the content area of the table.

2. Click the Insert Table button in the Insert bar, as shown in Figure 6-24.

Figure 6–24: Click the Insert Table button to insert a table.

3. In the Table dialog box that opens, choose the options for the new table:

- **Rows:** How many horizontal rows will appear in the table.

- **Columns:** How many vertical columns will appear in the table.

- **Table Width:** How wide the table will be in pixels or percentage. (If Percentage is chosen, the cell will stretch the indicated percentage to fit the available space.)

- **Border Thickness:** The thickness of the table borders. If 0 (zero) is chosen, the borders will be invisible (a common practice).

- **Cell Padding:** Adds spacing inside the cell (between the cell and the contents).

- **Cell Spacing:** Adds spacing outside the cell (between cells).

- **Header:** Formats one single row, column, or both as a header. Headers assist people using screen readers.

4. Enter the settings for the new table. Figure 6-25 shows that we are creating a three-column layout. If you wanted to enter the text directly into the cells, it would be a good idea to set some Cell Padding so that the text doesn't touch the edges of the cell. If you want to insert images that are flush against each other, choose a setting of 0.

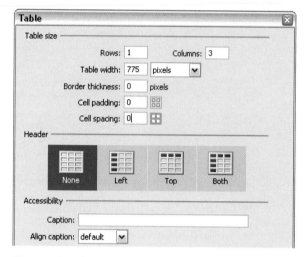

Figure 6–25: The settings for a three-column layout.

WARNING

If you do not physically type **0** into the border and cell settings, the default setting of 1 pixel is used for each option.

Figure 6-26 shows the new table inserted on the web page.

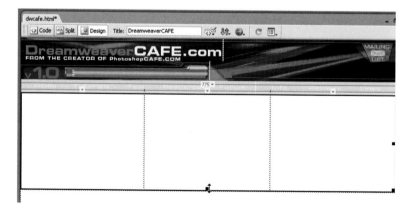

Figure 6–26: Resizing the cells.

Click and drag to resize any of the rows or columns, as shown in Figure 6–27. You may have to drag borders around a little bit to make everything fit correctly. You can also enter dimensions into the Property Inspector.

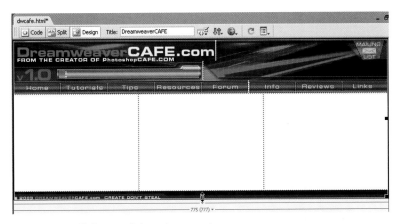

Figure 6–27: Clicking and dragging to resize.

The Design view provides a basic WYSIWYG (What You See Is What You Get) view of the page (Pronounced "wizzie-wig"). Sometimes what you see is not *exactly* what you get, though, so you should regularly preview your page in a web browser. To preview in the browser, press the F12 key. Your page will be launched in the web browser, as shown in Figure 6–28.

Figure 6–28: Testing in the web browser.

COLORIZING TABLES

You can use HTML to colorize tables or individual cells. By doing this, you can create a page that loads a lot faster than a page full of images. It's simple to colorize tables.

1. Click the cell you want to colorize. For multiple cells, click and drag with the mouse to select them all.

2. In the Property Inspector, click the box to the right of Bgcolor (bg on the Mac). You will see a pop-up Color palette. Choose the desired color, as shown in Figure 6-29. The hexadecimal number will be shown in the color field. You can also enter the hex numbers directly if you want.

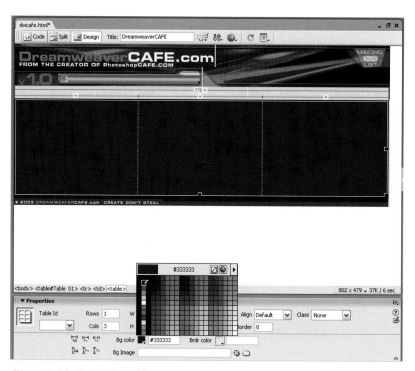

Figure 6–29: Colorizing tables.

CREATING CUSTOM CONTENT BOXES IN PHOTOSHOP/DREAMWEAVER

If you create a box in Dreamweaver, it will be pretty simple—basically not much more than a colored rectangle. You can create custom boxes with rounded corners, bevels, and irregularly shaped edges by using custom content boxes.

A content box is basically a three-celled table:

- The top header area
- The middle area, where the image is set as a repeating background; you can enter text into the cell over the top of the image
- The bottom bar

To build the content box, we will take our design from Photoshop to ImageReady, slice it, and then export the images. We will then create tables in Dreamweaver and add the images.

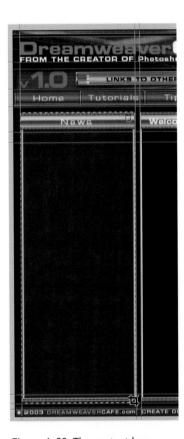

1. Open the layered layout comp in ImageReady. (We created the content images in previous chapters. If you didn't create them yet, create them now.) Figure 6-30 shows one of the content boxes.

Figure 6-30: The content box.

> **TIP**
>
> To launch a page in ImageReady from Photoshop, press the bottom-most button on the toolbox.

2. Choose the Slice tool and divide the content box into four slices. One slice (slice 01) should be the exact size of the header, and another (slice 04) should be used for the footer.

3. Slice 02 (as shown in Figure 6–31) will be the middle slice. Choose a small section; since this will be a repeating background, there is no need to select the entire content box. Choosing a smaller section and allowing it to repeat will cut down on the file size. (We will not be using slice 03.)

4. Open the Slice palette, select the first slice, and name it *content_L-top*, as shown in Figure 6–31.

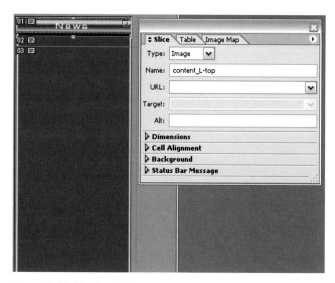

Figure 6–31: Naming a slice.

5. Choose the Slice Select tool and select slice 02. Name it *content_L-middle*.

6. Choose slice 04 and name it *content_L-bottom*. Don't bother naming slice 03 since we will not be needing it.

7. Choose the optimization settings for each slice. (Refer to Chapter 5 for more on optimization.)

Exporting Select Slices from ImageReady

Now let's export the sliced images from ImageReady. We don't want to export all the images on the page or the code, just the three images that we have prepared (top, middle, and bottom).

1. Choose the Slice Select tool and select the first slice.

2. Hold down the SHIFT key and click all the slices that you want to export (01, 02, and 04). All the selected slices will be highlighted, as shown in Figure 6-32.

3. Choose File | Save Optimized and enter the settings in the dialog box shown in Figure 6-33.

Figure 6–32: Select the slices to export.

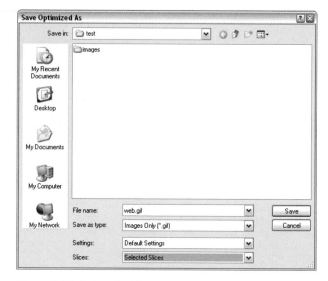

Figure 6–33: Saving the file.

4. Choose your home folder as the destination in the Save In (Where, on the Mac) field.

5. In the Save As Type (Format, on the Mac) field, choose Images Only. This will prevent any HTML pages from being written.

6. Select Selected Slices from the Slices drop-down. Now only the sliced images that we selected will be exported.

CREATING THE TABLES IN DREAMWEAVER

Go back to Dreamweaver and place the cursor in the call where you want to add the content box. We will create a new nested table.

1. Click the Insert Table button on the Insert bar.

2. In the Table dialog, choose the settings shown in Figure 6–34. For the Table Width, choose the same width as the slices that we exported. Set the Rows to 3 and the Columns to 1. Enter **0** for the rest of the settings.

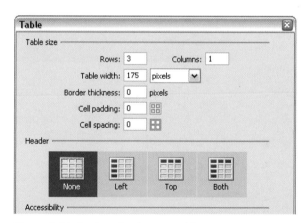

Figure 6–34: Settings for the new table.

Figure 6–35: The new table.

3. The table will appear as shown in Figure 6-35.

INSERTING THE IMAGES

Now let's place the images inside the table to give them a pleasant appearance.

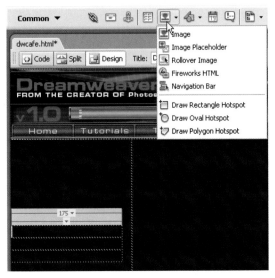

Figure 6–36: Inserting an image.

1. Place the cursor inside the top cell of the new table.

2. Choose the Common menu from the Insert bar, as shown in Figure 6-36; click the Image button, and then select Image from the drop-down menu.

3. You will see a new dialog box that will allow you to choose an image. Find the content_L-top image. When you click the image, you will see a preview to the right, as shown in Figure 6-37.

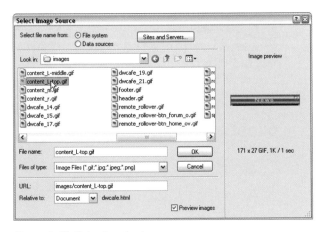

Figure 6–37: Selecting the image.

4. Click OK to insert the image.

5. Place the cursor in the bottom cell, and repeat steps 2–3 to insert the content_L-bottom image.

Centering the Table

To center the table:

1. Select the entire table by clicking outside it and dragging over it with the mouse.

2. In the Property Inspector's Align field, choose Center, as shown in Figure 6–38. This will center the table in its cell.

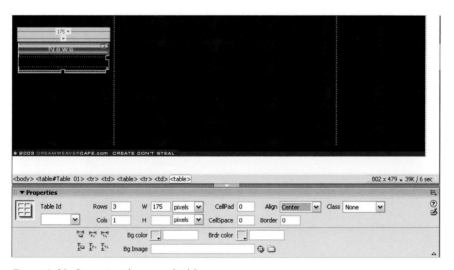

Figure 6–38: Centering the nested table.

Setting an Image as a Repeating Background

We have now created the top and bottom of our content box, but the center is still empty. We will choose the third slice as the background image. This way, we will be able to add text and other content over the top of it.

1. Place the cursor inside the middle cell, as shown in Figure 6–39.

2. In the Property Inspector, you'll see a field called Bg. You now have two options: either select the folder icon and navigate to the image, or try this cooler option—click the target icon and hold down your mouse button and drag to the image file (content_L-middle) in the Files palette.

Figure 6–39: Selecting the middle cell.

Figure 6–40: Choosing the background image.

You can see in Figure 6-40 that a line will follow the mouse as you target an image.

Figure 6–41: The image assigned as a background.

3. The image's name and path will be added to the Bg field, as shown in Figure 6-41.

The image will now be assigned as a background and will tile to fill the available space.

Figure 6–42: Adjusting the width of the table.

4. Click and drag with the mouse to make everything fit correctly. You may have to pull in the sides a little if they shifted while you inserted the images. In Figure 6-42, the width of the table is being dragged to get a snug fit.

5. Click and drag the bottom bar of the middle cell to stretch the height of the content box, as shown in Figure 6-43. You could also set the height and width (in pixels) in the Property Inspector.

Figure 6–43: Increasing the height of the content box.

Figure 6–44: Aligning the table to the top.

Figure 6–45: Notice the overlap of text over the left box border.

6. Select the content box, and in the Property Inspector, set its Vertical alignment to Top. This will make the nested table sit at the top of its host table, as shown in Figure 6-44.

7. You can now enter text into the content box. There is only one problem—notice that the text touches the left border, and this causes the text to overlap the images and look unpleasant, as shown in Figure 6-45. The solution to this problem is to nest yet another table.

8. Choose the Insert Table button, and in the Table dialog, box, enter **1** for both Rows and Columns, as shown in Figure 6-46. Choose 100 Percent for the Table Width and add a Cell Padding of 5 pixels. The cell padding will add some space around the text. (We are using a

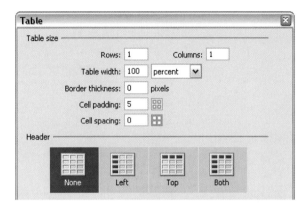

Figure 6–46: The table options.

nested table with the padding settings because if we set the padding of the original table, it would create gaps between the images.)

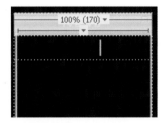

Figure 6–47: The text box provides some spacing around the text.

9. Now enter some text and notice in Figure 6-47 that space appears around it.

FORMATTING THE TEXT

Unfortunately, we can't see the text used here because it's almost the same color as the background. We can fix this by formatting the text:

1. Select the text.

2. Choose a font family from the Font field. For my site, I chose Arial, Helvetica, Sans-Serif. The web browser will look for the first available font on the visitors' computer. If it can't find Arial, it will search for and use Helvetica instead.

3. To change the text color, click in the text color box, as shown in Figure 6-48.

4. Select a color from the pop-up palette. Notice in Figure 6-49 that the button will change to the selected color of the text (white in this case). The corresponding

Figure 6–48: Choosing the text color.

hexadecimal number will also be displayed. Note that we have also centered the text and have top-aligned the nested table.

Figure 6–49: The color assigned to the text.

5. View the page, and you can see that the top of the box looks a bit too close to the navigation bar. Place the cursor to the left of the content box, and we'll add a line space.

6. If you press the ENTER key, by default a double space will be added. This is the new paragraph tag in HTML: <p></p>. To add a single space, hold down the SHIFT key and press ENTER. A <br> tag will be inserted instead, and a single space will appear above the content box. (Look in code or split view to see the HTML tags.) Figure 6-50 shows the final content box with white text and correct spacing.

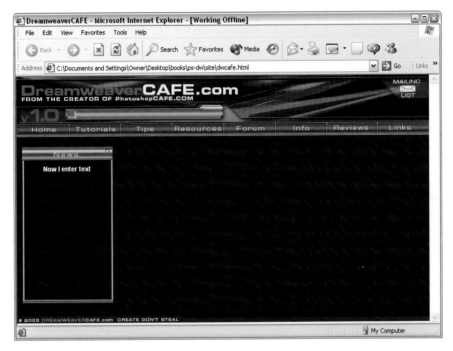

Figure 6–50: The final content box.

CREATING THE OTHER TWO CONTENT BOXES

Now that we have walked through the creation of the content box, you can repeat those steps for the next box to the right. Create the slices and name them, as shown in Figure 6–51. Take special care to make sure that the widths are the same for all the slices or you will have trouble assembling the final box.

Figure 6–51: Slicing the right box.

Repeat the steps for the middle box. Figure 6-52 shows the middle box with the slices selected ready for exporting.

Figure 6-53 shows the page with all the content boxes inserted. Choose the cells that host the content boxes and enter a width for each one in the Property Inspector, as shown in Figure 6-53. This is how we horizontally space the boxes.

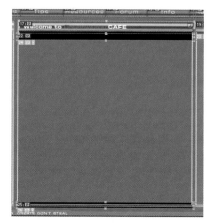

Figure 6–52: The middle box.

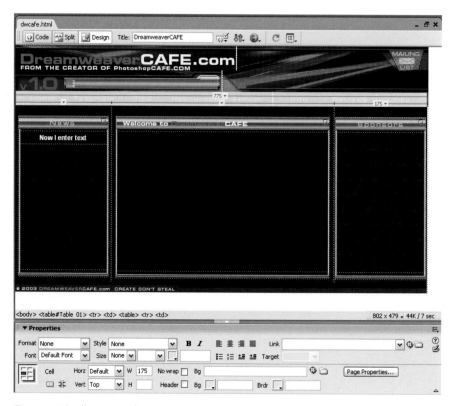

Figure 6–53: The content boxes assembled in the page.

FINISHING UP AND SETTING ALIGNMENT

To complete the content boxes:

1. Add the nested tables for the text and add some sample text to assist with alignment.

2. Click and drag the bottom of the text boxes down to expand their size, as shown in Figure 6-54.

Figure 6–54: Expanding the size of the text boxes.

3. Now align the text with the top of the boxes (vertical justification). Choose the text and then set the Alignment to Top in the Property Inspector, as shown in Figure 6-55.

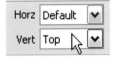

Figure 6–55: Setting the text alignment for the top.

Figure 6-56 shows the final page. All the boxes are ready for content. View the page in your browser to make sure everything looks OK (press F12). In the next chapter, we will look at turning the page into a site of pages.

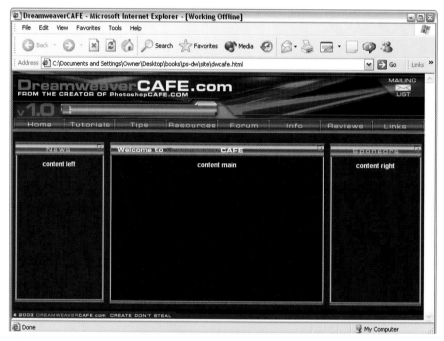

Figure 6–56: The final page displayed in a web browser.

CHAPTER 7

STREAMLINING THE PROCESS— USING CASCADING STYLE SHEETS AND TEMPLATES

Cascading style sheets (CSS) and the Dreamweaver template simplify the process of building a web site. In this chapter, we'll use a template to create web pages and CSS to style the content. This chapter deals with setting up the site; when we populate the site with content in the next chapter, you will see how much time you can save by creating style sheets and templates up front. Using these nifty time-saving tools can virtually eliminate repetitive tasks.

CASCADING STYLE SHEETS

CSS is a revolutionary web technology that defines the appearance of web pages; you can use CSS to position elements on a page and to format the appearance of text.

> **NOTE**
>
> Positioning page elements is outside the scope of this book; I have chosen the table positioning method instead because CSS positioning is still not compatible with all web browsers. You can find plenty of information about CSS positioning in Dreamweaver's online help.

Prior to CSS, the only way to change the appearance of text was to define a font tag and options every time some text was displayed. This resulted in code-bloated and messy HTML files—and, of course, a lot of work for web designers. Using strictly HTML, web designers had to format each piece of text separately. This could be a lot of work, especially for text-heavy, large sites. If text formatting needed to be changed at a later date, every instance of that text would have to be reformatted by hand. This is not the case with CSS. By simply changing the CSS file, every instance of the text can be updated across the entire site. I can't tell you how much time this has saved me in the real world. For example, I recently designed a site and formatted all the headings as orange. When I showed it to the client, he decided that blue would make him happier. All I had to do was update the style sheet to make the headers blue. The whole process took me about a minute. I didn't even have to open the pages I wanted updated!

How CSS Works

Cascading style sheets work much like the text styles you apply in your favorite word processor. You choose all the characteristics of a style and then apply it to text with a few clicks.

For the web, two types of CSS are used:

- **Embedded:** All the settings are embedded in the header of the HTML page. By default, Dreamweaver MX 2004 converts formatting to CSS.

- **External style sheet:** All the formatting is stored in an external file with a .css extension. This page is referenced by the individual pages, and the formatting is applied to all the linked pages. This is called *global formatting*.

CSS is called *cascading* because the formatting is applied in a cascading fashion; the external style sheet supplies all the page formatting, the embedded tags will override the external formatting; and local formatting will override the other options. This makes it easy to format a page and then apply tweaks locally.

> **NOTE**
>
> Because of the cascading format, when the global styles are updated, local formatting will be unchanged.

Advantages of CSS

There are several advantages of using CSS over HTML:

- **Uniform appearance:** Because all the pages share the same master style sheet, their appearance will be uniform.

- **Tighter, more integrated code:** The CSS classes are much cleaner than HTML font tags; this also makes for more streamlined, faster downloading pages.

- **Quickly set up the appearance of pages:** Instead of individually choosing all the characteristics of text, simply attach a style.

- **Easy and fast updating of pages:** Update the CSS information and the entire site is updated.

- **More control than HTML:** Characteristics are available in CSS that are not available in HTML.

TIP

If your styles don't appear on the page, make sure you restore all local formatting to the default settings. Select all the text and from the Properties Inspector, choose "none" for Format.

Creating Your First CSS Style

Without further introduction, let's jump into our project and set up a style sheet:

1. Open your working project. Whether it looks like the example here or totally different doesn't matter; the principles are the same.

Figure 7–1: Sample text.

2. Add some sample text for the body and header, as shown in Figure 7-1. (This is not the final text; it simply gives you a visual cue to the existing formatting.)

3. Remove all formatting from the text. To do this, select the text; then, in the Property Inspector, choose None from both the Style and Format drop-down menus.

4. Open the CSS Styles panel from the Window Menu (choose Window | CSS Styles), or select the CSS Styles tab from the Design Panel if it's open.

5. Click the Create New Style button at the bottom of the Styles panel to create a new CSS Style, as shown in Figure 7-2. The New CSS Style dialog box will open.

6. Now let's define our first style, starting with the body text format. In the dialog box, choose Class for the Selector Type.

7. Under Name, enter **.body**, as shown in Figure 7-3. Make sure that you add the period before the name; this is the correct naming format for CSS styles.

Figure 7–2: Creating a new style.

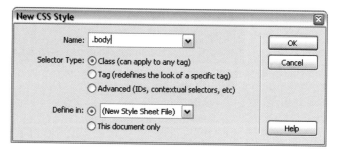

Figure 7–3: Creating a new style sheet.

8. For the Define In option, choose New Style Sheet.

9. Click OK. We will now have the opportunity to save the style sheet. This will create a separate document. We will use this CSS document to format our site. The first time you define a style, a new CSS document will be created. Choose the root directory of your web site and name the style sheet. In Figure 7-4, the style sheet is named dwcafe.css. This style sheet is a separate document that we will use to format our site.

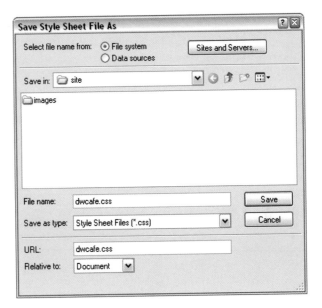

Figure 7–4: Naming the style sheet.

10. Click Save to save the style sheet. (This option will appear only when you are creating a new style sheet.)

> **NOTE**
>
> A new CSS document will open in Dreamweaver as soon as you save it. This is our master style sheet for this site.

11. Continue formatting your style sheet in the CSS Style Definition dialog box.

12. Under Category, choose Type and then choose your text preferences and color, as shown in Figure 7-5. This sets up the appearance of the body tag.

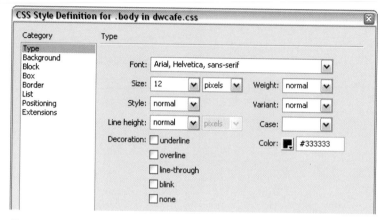

Figure 7–5: Formatting the text.

13. In the CSS Styles tab of the Design pane, you'll see the CSS file you just created. Click the box to the left of the filename (the box shows a plus sign in Windows and an arrow on the Mac) to expand the style, and you will see a body tag, as shown in Figure 7-6.

Figure 7–6: The CSS Styles tab of the Design palette.

DEFINING A NEW TAG IN AN EXISTING STYLE SHEET

Now let's set up a new style for the heading.

1. Click the Create New Style button in the CSS Styles tab, as you did in the preceding section.

2. When the New CSS Style dialog box opens, enter **.head** into the Name field, as shown in Figure 7-7. This is the name of your heading style.

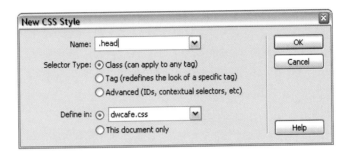

Figure 7–7: Entering the name for the heading style.

3. Click OK, and the CSS Style Definition window will open.

4. Choose the Type category and enter the settings for the heading text formatting, as shown in Figure 7-8.

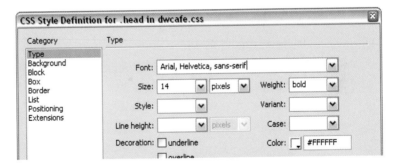

Figure 7–8: Settings for the heading style.

5. Click OK to apply the style.

We have now defined two styles for the head and the body.

ATTACHING A STYLE SHEET TO YOUR HTML PAGE

After you have created a style sheet, you can attach it to any HTML document. You can even reuse style sheets for different web sites.

Figure 7–9: Attach style sheet button.

1. In the Design palette, click the attach style sheet button, shown in Figure 7-9.

2. You will see two options: Link and Import. Choose Link to attach an external style sheet, and click the Browse button, as shown in Figure 7-10.

Figure 7–10: Clicking the Browse button.

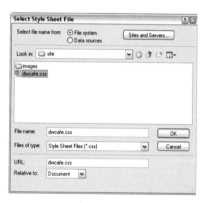

3. In the Select Style Sheet File dialog box, locate your saved style sheet and select it, as shown in Figure 7-11.

4. Click OK, and the style sheet is attached to the HTML page and ready for use.

Figure 7–11: Selecting the style sheet.

USING THE STYLE SHEET

It's now a simple process to style the text using the attached style sheets. In the Property Inspector, you'll see a Style drop-down menu. We'll use this to apply the styles.

1. Select the text in the Design Window by clicking and dragging across it.

2. Choose a style from the Style drop-down menu. Figure 7-12 shows applying the head style, and Figure 7-13 shows the web page with some styles added.

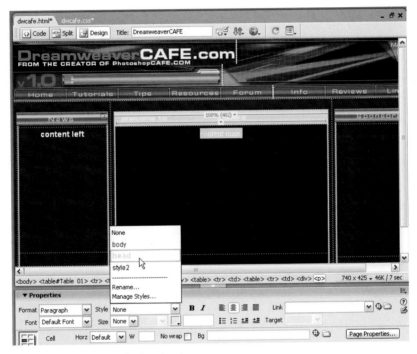

Figure 7-12: Applying the head style.

Figure 7-13: The Head styles applied to the content boxes.

MODIFYING STYLE SHEETS

After a style is applied to text, you can modify it at any time. You can either modify the text from the Property Inspector, which will affect only the page you are working on (local change), or you can modify the style sheet. When you modify the style sheet, every instance of the style, site-wide, will be updated to reflect the modifications.

1. Open the Tag Inspector—choose Window | Tag Inspector.

2. Click the Relevant CSS tab.

3. In the Design palette, open the CSS Styles panel.

4. Choose the style you want to modify from the CSS Styles panel; the Relevant CSS tab will update to show all the available characteristics for the chosen style. In this case, let's work on the body tag.

5. Find Font-Size and click just to the right; drop-down options will appear, as shown in Figure 7-14. Choose 11 pixels.

List view

Category view

Notice in Figure 7-15 how the site type has updated to match the style sheet.

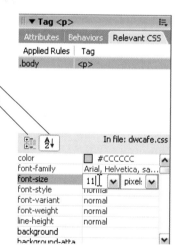

Figure 7–14: The Relevant CSS panel.

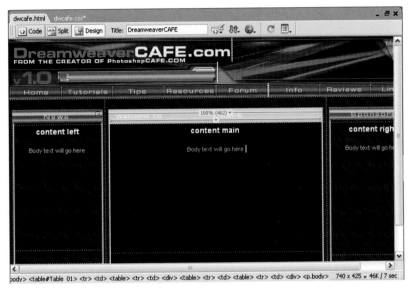

Figure 7–15: The updated styles on the page.

6. All the text is currently centered; let's change the alignment to left. Choose Block from the Relevant CSS panel. (Choose Category view.)

7. Find Text-Align and change it to Left, as shown in Figure 7-16.

Figure 7-17 shows how all three instances of the body text are updated and all are aligned left. This method is a lot faster than updating each piece of text individually.

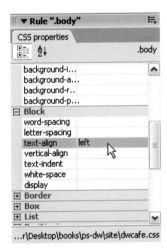

Figure 7–16: Changing the text alignment.

Figure 7–17: The updated page.

8. A little more space between the text and the edge of the box is needed, so let's fix that now. Back in Chapter 6, we set the cell padding. Because we are going to inset the text with CSS in this procedure, change the Cell Padding back to 0.

9. In the CSS Properties tab, find the Text-Indent box and enter a setting of 5 pixels, as shown in Figure 7-18.

When you test the page in a web browser, as shown in Figure 7-19, notice that spacing appears between the text and the cell border, and all the text is formatted to your specifications.

Figure 7–18: Setting the text indent.

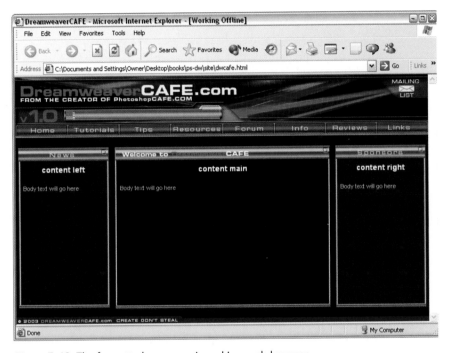

Figure 7–19: The formatted page previewed in a web browser.

> **TIP**
>
> Press F12 to preview the page in your favorite web browser.

TEMPLATES

Templates are another wonderful way to save time: when you create a page, you can define it as a template, and then the design can be applied to any page with a single click. Moreover, if you make a change to the template, every page on the site that uses the template will also be updated. When a template is applied to a page, it is locked so that nothing can be moved around by accident.

You can define regions as *editable*, which means they can be changed and are not locked. These editable regions are where you will put your content and the rest of the page will remain locked.

> **TIP**
>
> To make a template-generated page fully editable, choose: Modify | Templates | Detach From Template. Note that once you do this, the page will not be updated when the template is updated because the page will now be an independent html page.

Converting a Page to a Template

It's a simple task to convert a page to a template. It's a good idea to attach the style sheet to the template first so that the style sheet is automatically attached to every page generated by the template.

1. With your desired page open, choose File | Save As Template.

2. Make sure that the working site is selected in the Site window.

Figure 7–20: Saving a template.

3. Choose a name for the template and save it. In Figure 7-20, the template is named *main*, since this will be our main template in the site. (The page will be assigned a .dwt extension.)

4. If the Update Links dialog box opens, choose Update to apply the template changes to the Child (Created From The Template) pages. If you don't want to update the child pages, click Don't Update.

The entire page is now saved as a template. When you create a new document from the template, you will not be able to enter any text or make changes except in regions you have defined as editable.

> **NOTE**
>
> The template itself will always be editable, and the changes will be broadcast throughout all the pages that contain the template.

DEFINING A TABLE AS AN EDITABLE REGION

Let's make the three content boxes editable. We'll start on the middle content box, or table. We will use tag selectors to select the entire table.

1. Click inside the middle content table.

2. At the bottom of the content table, you will see a list of HTML tags. Choose the `<table>` tag that is the closest to the right, as shown in Figure 7–21. (The tags on the left are for the parent tables.)

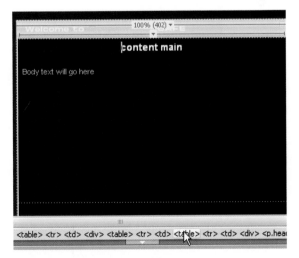

Figure 7–21: Selecting the table tag.

3. The content table should now be selected, as shown in Figure 7-22.

4. From the Insert bar, choose the Common option.

5. Click the Template icon, and you will see a drop-down menu, as shown in Figure 7-23. Choose the Editable Region option.

Figure 7–22: The selected table.

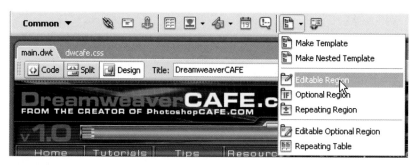

Figure 7–23: Making a region editable.

6. A dialog box asks for the name of the new editable region. It's important that you give the region a meaningful name, because you may include several editable regions on a page.

7. Name the region *middle*, as shown in Figure 7-24, and click OK.

8. Repeat steps 1–7 for the left table. Name it *left,* as shown in Figure 7-25.

Figure 7–24: Naming the middle region.

Figure 7–25: Naming the left region.

9. Define a region for the right content table and name it *right.*

10. Choose Save to save the changes to the template.

If you look in the Files panel you will see that a folder called Templates has been created. All the templates created for the site are stored in this folder. You can see the main.dwt file in the Templates folder, as shown in Figure 7-26.

Figure 7–26:
The templates folder.

MACROMEDIA CONTRIBUTE

Templates are the best way to work if you are using the Macromedia Contribute application. Contribute allows members of a web team to add and change content on a site while maintaining the site integrity. By using templates, non-technical users can update content of a site without using code or databases, and templates can prevent folks from making design changes or damaging code.

Using Templates

Now that we have created a template, let's generate a new page from the new template.

1. Choose File | New.

2. In the New dialog box, select the Templates tab.

3. Select a site (DreamweaverCAFE, in our case).

4. Select a template from those that appear in the middle window. In our case, only one template is available—main, as shown in Figure 7–27.

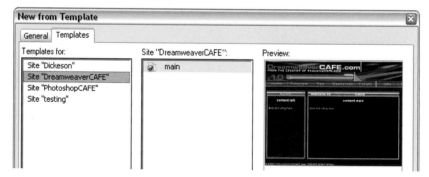

Figure 7–27: Creating a new page from a template.

5. Double-click the template name, or select the template and click the Create button.

The new page will be created and will look just like the template that we created earlier. This is a fast way to create new pages.

6. Save the page right away. Note that you must name it the same as the homepage link we created when we first designed the page, or it won't work. Name it index.htm and save it in our site root, as shown in Figure 7–28.

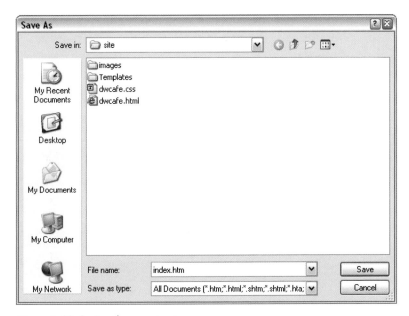

Figure 7–28: Saving the new page.

ADDING CONTENT

Notice that if you move your mouse over the template, a circle with a line in it appears. This is the international sign for "No," as shown in Figure 7-29. This means that you cannot edit this template because it is locked.

Figure 7–29: You cannot change a locked template.

1. Move your mouse over the regions that you defined as editable. Notice that the No sign does not appear; you can edit these areas.

2. Type some text into the editable content areas, as shown in Figure 7-30.

Figure 7–30: Adding text into the editable region.

3. Save the page.

4. Press the F12 key to display the page in a web browser.

If you update the template, all the added content will be unaffected; only the locked template regions will be updated. This is a super-fast way to update the look of your entire site.

CREATING HYPERLINKS

Hyperlinks are HTML's way of moving around the Internet. When a user clicks a hyperlink, he or she is sent to another place on the page, to another page on the same site, or to a totally different site. Let's create a hyperlink and then style it using templates.

Creating Text Hyperlinks

Let's start by creating hyperlinked text on the page:

Figure 7–31: Choosing the text.

1. Choose the text you want to use as a hyperlink by clicking and dragging, as shown in Figure 7-31.

2. In the Property Inspector Link field, type in the link address. If you want to go to a page on the current site, enter the name of the page: for example, enter *page***.htm**. To go off the site, start with *http://,* as shown in Figure 7-32.

Figure 7–32: Entering an offsite hyperlink.

3. Assign a Target, which controls how the web browser will handle opening the new page. If you are using frames, the target will allow you to control in which frame the page will be opened.

The description from the help file in Dreamweaver describes targets as follows:

- **_blank:** Opens the linked document in a new browser window, leaving the current window untouched.

- **_parent:** Opens the linked document in the parent frameset of the frame in which the link appears, replacing the entire frameset.

- **_self:** Opens the link in the current frame, replacing the content in that frame.

- **_top:** Opens the linked document in the current browser window, replacing all frames.

4. If you are not using frames, leaving the Target field blank will open the links in the same window. Choosing **_blank**, as shown in Figure 7-33, or typing **_blank** or **new**, will open a new browser window with the target page.

Figure 7–33: Setting the link to open in a new window.

TIP

As a rule, I open a new window for offsite links; this way, when the viewer closes the links window, the host site is still displayed on the desktop, thus retaining visitors. I also try to open links within the site in the same window and thus reduce clutter from pop-ups.

Figure 7-34 shows the hyperlink added to the page. This is the default appearance for a link. To change it, read on.

Figure 7-34: The added hyperlink.

TIP

If you want to link to a specific place on a page, you must first define an anchor. Click in the desired location of the page, choose Insert I Named Anchor, and then assign a name. To jump to an anchor on the same page as the hyperlink, enter a # symbol and then the name. For example, you would enter **#goHere** to jump to the anchor on the same page as the hyperlink; if the link is on another page, you'd enter *page.htm#goHere*.

Changing the Appearance of a Hyperlink

Let's change the way that the hyperlinks are displayed. We can change the color of the links and even cause the color to change as the mouse rolls over the link. We'll make the change to the template; this way, we can be sure that all the links on the site are consistent.

NOTE

We could change the appearance of the links using CSS (see "Modifying the Appearance of Links Using CSS" later in this chapter), but for now we will change the template so that you can learn about page properties and updating templates.

---

1. Open your template in Dreamweaver.

2. Choose Modify | Page Properties (or press CTRL-J in Windows; CMD-J on Mac). The Page Properties dialog box will open.

3. Choose the Links category.

4. Select colors for the four states:

   • **Link Color:** The color of a hyperlink on the page

   • **Visited Links:** The color of a previously visited link

   • **Rollover Links:** The color of the link as the mouse rolls over it

   • **Active Links:** The color of a link as it is clicked

5. Click the Underline Style drop-down arrow to set the underline options. The settings shown in Figure 7–35 will not show the underline on rollovers.

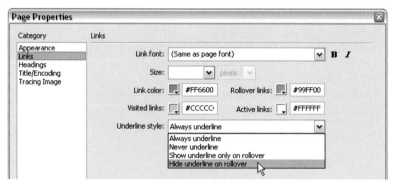

Figure 7–35: Setting hyperlink options.

6. Click OK to apply.

7. Click File | Save to save the template.

8. In the Update Template Files dialog box shown in Figure 7-36, you're asked whether you want to update all the pages using the template. If you want to apply the changes to all the pages using the template, click Update; otherwise, click Don't Update. You can also select the pages from the list that you wish to update. To select more than one page at a time, hold down CTRL (CMD on the Mac) as you click.

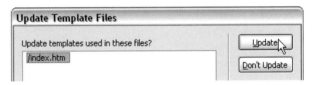

Figure 7-36: Updating the template pages.

9. You will see a list of the pages as they are updated. A confirmation will be displayed, which says "Done," as shown in Figure 7-37.

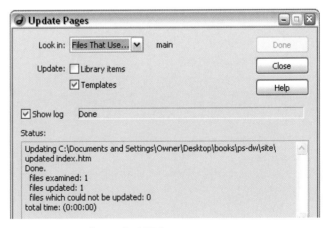

Figure 7-37: Updating the HTML pages.

In Figure 7–38A, you can see the updated hyperlinks on your page when it's previewed in a browser. Notice that as you roll over a link in Figure 7–38B, the color changes and the underline disappears. This is a quick and easy way to add a bit of interactivity to a site.

Figure 7–38: The link on the page (A); the link as the mouse rolls over it (B).

A–Link

B–Rollover

MODIFYING THE APPEARANCE OF LINKS USING CSS

CSS gives you a great deal of control over the appearance of a page. You can also redefine how links will look on a page.

1. Create a new style by clicking the Create New Style button at the bottom of the Styles panel.

2. In the New CSS Style dialog box, choose the Advanced option, as shown in Figure 7-39.

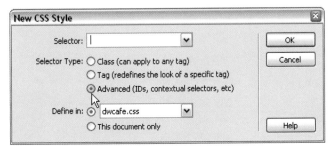

Figure 7–39: Redefining the advanced type.

3. Click the Selector drop-down arrow, and you will see the different rollover states. Choose one to modify its properties, as shown in Figure 7-40.

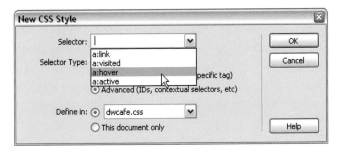

Figure 7–40: Choosing the link state.

4. The CSS Style Definition box will open, as shown in Figure 7-41. Choose the categories and corresponding settings that you want to change.

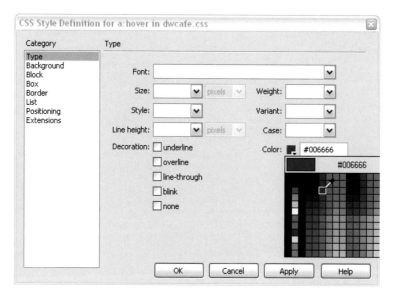

Figure 7–41: Redefining the links.

I suggest that only the colors of links be changed at this point. I don't like to change a font or its weight on a rollover because this can cause body text to reflow during the rollover, and trying to catch the link on these pages is like chasing butterflies. Many users will not bother with this hassle and will move on to a page that is easier to navigate. It's great to make your pages look great, but keep them functional!

CHAPTER 8

CREATING THE WHOLE SITE

You have learned how to create individual web pages and explored strategies for creating pages, such as using templates and cascading style sheets (CSS). Now that you have designed the templates and layouts for a web page and created the web page, you can create the rest of the pages in the web site.

After you build the site "skeleton"—the site map, templates, and CSS—your main design work is finished. In this chapter, you'll move on to the next step: populating web pages with content. Useful content will give people a reason to visit the site. Special content that is more of a resource, sometimes called *sticky* content, gives visitors a reason to return your web site.

THE SITE MAP

In Chapter 1 you created some sketches, including a *site map*—a flow chart of sorts that lists all the pages that will exist on your web site. You can have Dreamweaver create a site map for you. Although this map cannot be used to generate pages, it is a useful visual aid that helps you create the site. In this section, you'll use the site map to help you keep track of the various pages that will appear on your site. We'll look at three strategies you can use for creating pages.

Viewing the Site Map

Bring up the site map in Dreamweaver.

1. Open the Files panel, if it is not already open: choose Window | Files, or press F8.

2. Click the expander button, as shown in Figure 8-1.

3. On the top button bar are three buttons that contain little boxes. Click the third button, the site map button, and choose Map Only from the drop-down menu, as shown in Figure 8-2.

Figure 8-1: Expanding the Files panel.

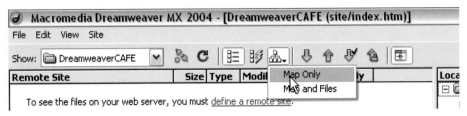

Figure 8–2: Choosing the Map Only option from the site map button.

The site map is displayed. The home page will appear on top of the map and the links will be shown on the next branch of the tree. Notice that the names of the pages are displayed in red, and a "broken chain" icon is displayed, as shown in Figure 8-3, indicating that the links are broken. (They are broken because these pages do not yet exist.) You will also notice a link displayed in blue type with a globe logo. This indicates that the link is offsite (on another web page).

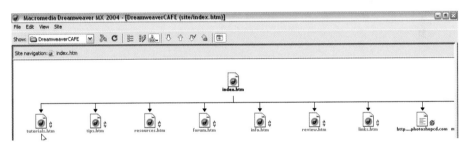

Figure 8–3: Site map showing broken links.

SETTING THE HOME PAGE

You can choose which page you want to set as the top (home page) in the site map hierarchy and change it from the default if you wish. This is useful if you are working on sites with multiple home pages or with directories several levels deep. You can simplify the site map for just the section you are working on.

1. From the Show drop-down menu in the Files panel, choose Manages Sites, as shown in Figure 8-4.

2. In the Site Definition window, choose the Advanced tab.

3. Select Site Map Layout from the Category list.

4. Next to the Home Page field, click the folder icon to navigate and choose the home page you want to use for the site map, as shown in Figure 8-5. The selected page will appear at the top of the site map.

Figure 8–4: Managing sites.

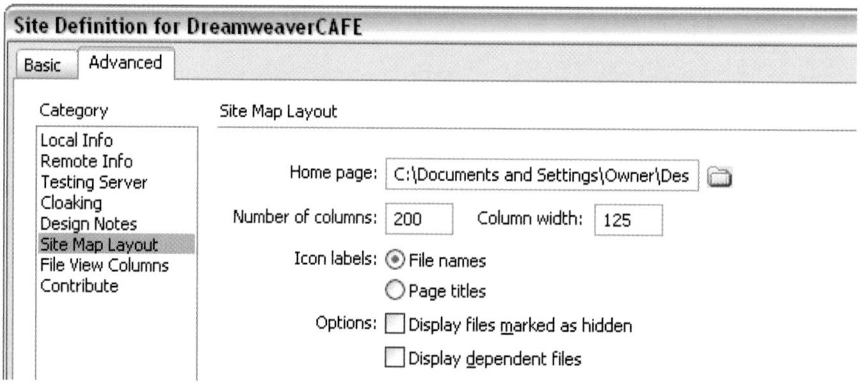

Figure 8–5: Setting a home page for the site map.

CREATING NEW PAGES

Now that you can view the site map and see the names of the missing pages, it's time to create the web pages on the site. You can use one of three methods to create pages.

Method 1: Creating Pages from the Files Panel

First, you need to change the view so that you can see the existing files and the site map at the same time.

1. Click the site map button from the button bar (the same button you chose earlier) and choose the Map And Files option. You'll see a split view of the map and files, as shown in Figure 8-6.

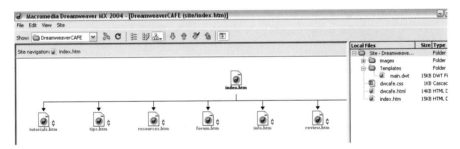

Figure 8–6: The map and files view.

2. Right-click (CONTROL-click) the top level folder in the files window on the right.

3. From the context menu, choose New File.

4. A new file named Untitled will appear in the files window. Enter a new name for the file—use the name of one of the files shown on the site map. In this case, type in **tips.htm**. You will notice that the site map will update to show the name of the link in black, as shown in Figure 8-7. This indicates that the page now exists.

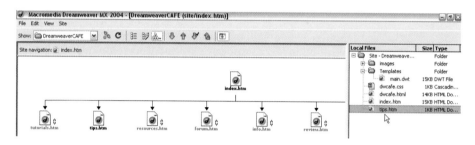

Figure 8–7: After the tips.htm page is created, it shows up in black in the site map.

5. Double-click the tips.htm page's icon in either the site map or the files window to open the page. Presently, the page is a blank HTML page.

6. Now apply the template to the page. Choose Modify | Templates | Apply Template To Page.

7. A dialog box will appear, displaying all the available templates. In this case, since you have created only a single template called main, choose the main template and click Select, as shown in Figure 8-8.

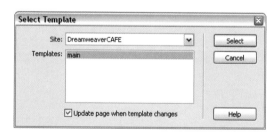

Figure 8–8: Selecting the template.

8. The template will be applied to the page, as shown in Figure 8-9. Save the page. You can now enter the desired page name into the title area and add content to the page.

Figure 8–9: The template applied to the page.

Method 2: Applying a Template to an Existing Page

You can also generate a new page by applying the template to existing content and then telling Dreamweaver where to place the content. This is a good method to use if you are applying the template to dress up a dull page. (In this case, you will create the page from scratch, so you will know how to do it.)

1. Choose File | New to create a new, blank web page.

2. In the New Document dialog box, choose the General tab.

3. Select Basic Page from the left window.

4. In the Basic Page window, choose HTML. Click Create.

5. A blank page is created. Insert some text, as shown in Figure 8-10. Choose File | Save As, and name the file—in this case, name it **tutorials.htm.** This page will appear after visitors click the Tutorials navigation button on your main page.

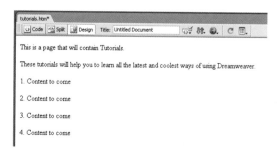

Figure 8–10: New page with text entered.

6. Now apply a template to the page. Choose Modify | Templates | Apply Template To Page.

7. In the Select Template dialog box, choose the template and click the Select button.

8. Because the page already contains some content, a new dialog box appears: the Inconsistent Region Names dialog box. A text message informs you that some regions in the document have no corresponding regions in the template. In

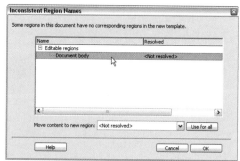

Figure 8–11: Dreamweaver doesn't know where to place the content.

English, this means "Some content already exists on the page; please tell me where to put it." The words *<Not resolved>* will appear in the Results column. Click this line to highlight it, as shown in Figure 8-11.

9. Click the down arrow next to Move Content To New Region. A drop-down menu will appear that contains all the editable regions, including the following:

- **Nowhere:** Discards all the content on the page
- **Doctitle:** Formats the text as a default editable region on all pages—in this case, the title of the page
- **Head:** Places the content into the header of the page (used mainly for coding purposes)
- **Left, Middle, and Right:** The editable regions that we created ourselves

  All the regions that you defined as editable when you created the template will appear here.

10. Select Middle to choose the large content box in the middle of the page, as shown in Figure 8-12.

11. Click OK. The text is placed inside the middle

Figure 8–12: Choosing the middle region to place content.

Figure 8–13: Content placed into the template.

content area on the template, as shown in Figure 8-13.

12. Now to format the text using CSS: in the middle content area, click and drag with the mouse to select all the text, just as you would if you were using a word processor, as shown in Figure 8-14.

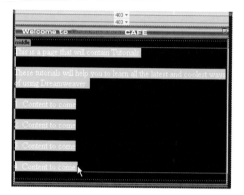

Figure 8–14: Selecting the text.

13. Because a style sheet was applied to the template, it will be available now for your page. From the Style drop-down menu in the Property Inspector, choose Body, as shown in Figure 8-15.

14. Apply the Head style to the heading of the text. Notice that the text in the heading is touching the edges on the left. It's good design sense to allow some space. You can modify this style.

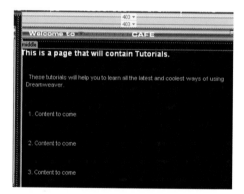

Figure 8–15: Applying the style to the content.

15. In the Design panel, click the .head style (or any style you wish to modify). Then click the pencil icon to modify the style, as shown in Figure 8-16.

16. From the CSS Style Definition dialog box, choose the attributes you want to

Figure 8–16: Choosing the style to modify.

modify. In this case, you are modifying the space between the text and the content area's margin. Choose the Box category, click the Same For All box under Padding and Margin and enter a setting of **10** for the Top field

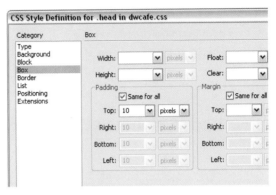

Figure 8–17: Setting the margin.

under Padding to apply a 10-pixel margin around all the text, as shown in Figure 8-17.

Figure 8–18: The finished page.

The text will now be inset correctly. Don't forget to save the style; when you do, the setting will be saved in the style and will be applied to all the pages in the site that are using this style. The finished page is shown in Figure 8-18.

Method 3: Renaming Existing Pages

This method for creating new pages is the fastest for pages that will use the same look and feel. This method works for pages with and without templates.

1. Open a page that you want to replicate.

2. Choose File | Save As.

3. Enter the name of the new page. As shown in Figure 8-19, type in the name **resources.htm**. (In this step for your own web pages, you will always choose the name of one of the uncreated pages from the site map.)

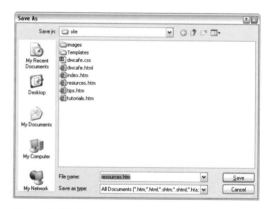

Figure 8–19: Creating a new page by duplicating an existing page.

4. Click Save and the new page is created. This page will use all the attributes of the original page, including templates and CSS. (Don't forget to change the page's title.)

Finishing Up

Continue using your preferred method to produce the rest of the pages that you need for your site.

> **TIP**
>
> Click the Refresh button in the File window to update the site map and see which pages still need to be created. Uncreated page names are shown in red type.

When you're done producing pages, press F12 to test the site in the browser. Click each of the navigation buttons to link to and open the corresponding page. Each time you click a button, the corresponding page should appear. If one of the links

Figure 8–20: The complete site.

is broken, open the site map and try to discover why—perhaps you misnamed a page or forgot to generate one.

You have now built a fully functional web site with working navigation buttons. The completed site is shown in Figure 8-20. Next, we'll look at different ways of bringing in content.

PLACING IMAGES IN DREAMWEAVER

You can place images inside your web pages, whether photos or other types of graphics. These can be saved as JPEG, GIF, or PNG files. Make sure that you optimize and save the images to the images folder from Photoshop/ImageReady.

Figure 8–21: Inserting the image.

1. Position the cursor on the page where you want to insert the image.

2. Click the Image button on the Insert bar and choose Image, as shown in Figure 8-21.

3. In the Select Image Source dialog box, find the images folder and locate your image. Click the image's name, and a preview appears on the right side of the window, as shown in Figure 8-22.

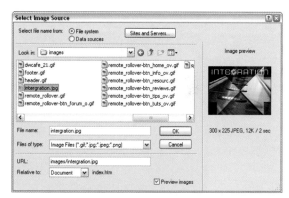

Figure 8–22: Selecting the image.

4. Click OK (Choose on the Mac) to insert the image. The images will appear on the page, as shown in Figure 8-23.

Figure 8–23: The inserted image.

TIP

To wrap text around an image, click the image, and then in the Property Inspector, choose Left or Right for the Alignment. The text will automatically wrap around the image.

IMPORTING TEXT INTO DREAMWEAVER

When you are building a web site, it's common to type in text content using a word processing program such as Microsoft Word. You can then cut and paste the text from Word into Dreamweaver. But there is an easier way to do this: the Word file can be imported directly into Dreamweaver. Here's how:

1. First create and save a Word document that contains the text you want to use in the site.

2. In Dreamweaver, click in the spot on the page where you want to place the text.

3. Choose File | Import | Word Document. Notice that options also appear for XML, Tabular Data, and Excel Document placement. (To bring such documents into Dreamweaver for the Mac, you will have to open the documents in their native programs, select all text, and copy it. Then open Dreamweaver and paste it into the page.)

Figure 8–24: The text placed in Dreamweaver.

4. Locate and select the document (in this case, a Word document) you want to import.

5. Click OK and the text will be imported into Dreamweaver, as shown in Figure 8-24. The original Word formatting will be retained as much as possible. In this case, though, we will reformat the text using CSS.

6. Highlight the text and apply the head and body styles to it, as shown in Figure 8-25.

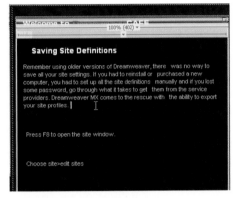

Figure 8-25: Styling the text.

Changing Line Spacing

You may have noticed overly large line breaks between paragraphs in the Dreamweaver document. You can modify these breaks.

1. Place the cursor at the end of the paragraph previous to the bad break and press the DELETE (DEL) key until the paragraph break has been removed and the next paragraph's text is located to the right of the cursor, as shown in Figure 8-26. (Compare Figure 8-25 with Figure 8-26 to see how the paragraphs were changed.)

Figure 8-26: Ready to apply a paragraph break.

2. By default, if you press the ENTER (RETURN) key, a double space will be applied according to Dreamweaver's default settings. To apply a single line space, hold down the SHIFT key and press ENTER (RETURN). The text will now have a single line space, as shown in Figure 8-27.

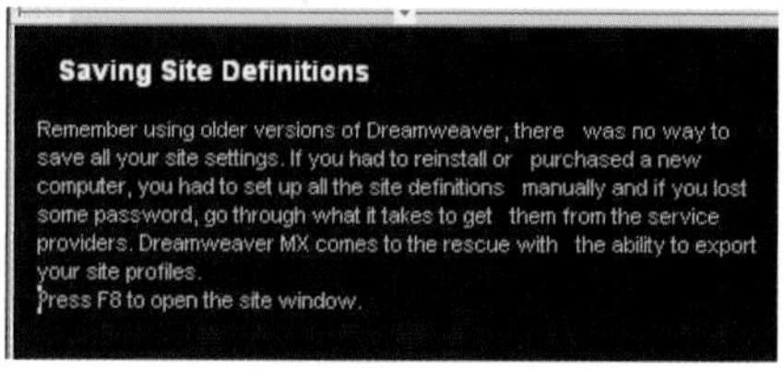

Figure 8–27: Adding a single line space.

TIP

Using the paragraph (ENTER or RETURN) key has a much more drastic effect on spacing in browsers. As a general rule, you should use single line spaces (SHIFT-ENTER or SHIFT-RETURN) instead.

---

3. To add another line break, press SHIFT-ENTER (SHIFT-RETURN). A double line space overrides the embedded style, as shown in Figure 8-28.

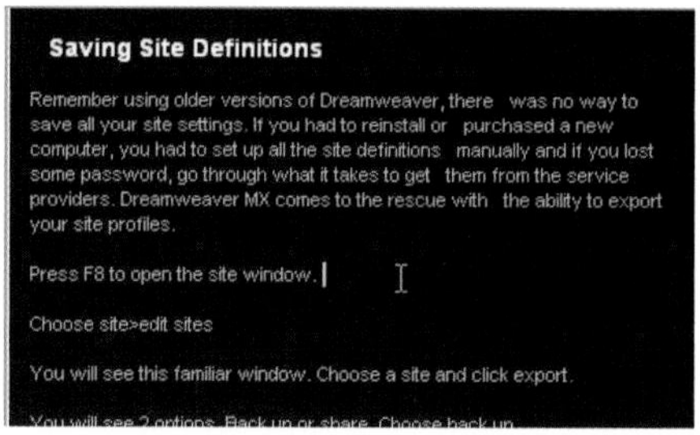

4. Continue formatting the text until you are happy with its appearance. Figure 8-29 shows the formatted text in the Dreamweaver web page.

Figure 8–28: Adding a double line space.

5. Using what you have learned so far, open each of the pages on your web site and insert all the text and images. This is called "populating" a site with content.

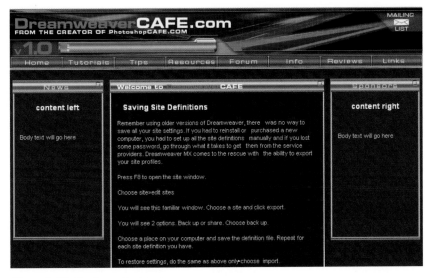

Figure 8–29: The formatted text.

You have finished building the basic site. In the next chapter, we'll add some inter-activity and look at some advanced uses of images.

CHAPTER 9

ADD MOVEMENT AND INTERACTIVITY

In this chapter we will explore those little things that make the page appear "alive." Interactive elements respond to user actions like rolling over an image with the mouse. Interactivity makes the user feel more involved in the site and enhances the surfing experience.

TRANSPARENCY

Have you ever seen irregularly shaped images on web sites? This is an illusion, because all images on web pages are actually rectangular in shape. Some of an image's pixels can, however, be made transparent, thus projecting the illusion of an image being of a non-rectangular shape, such as a circle or other irregular shape.

You may be asking, "Why not just create a shape with a background color that matches the HTML background color?" The biggest reason for not doing this is because not all backgrounds are solid colors. For example, you may want to place an image on top of a patterned background or over an image. A transparent image's background allows the page background to display through so that the image appears to have no visible border around it. Without transparency, a border will appear around the image, but when saved with transparency the image will appear to float against the page background.

Two file formats support transparency: GIF and PNG. If you don't need to include any semitransparent pixels (one level of transparency—either solid or transparent), GIF is the best choice. If you need varying levels of transparency, use PNG. The process of creating the transparent file is exactly the same for both formats, but PNG files are larger than GIF files. Let's take a look at the workflow and best strategies to use for creating transparent images for the Web.

Preparing the Image

If an image background is to appear transparent on the Web, you must create some areas of transparency in ImageReady. In the Layers palette, you can hide an image background by clicking the eye icon to the left of the background layer name, as shown here.

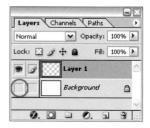

If the image is flat and "background" is the only layer, then you will have to convert it to a layer. Double-click the word "background" and click OK when the New Layer dialog box appears. You can now erase parts of the image to transparency.

> **NOTE:**
>
> You must create a layer before you can hide its background.

Alternatively, when you first create the new document, choose Transparent for its background color in the New Document dialog box. Figure 9-1 shows an image with transparency: the checkerboard pattern indicates the transparency around the circle image.

Photoshop can detect the edges of the image's pixels and trim away all the unneeded image area. Using Photoshop's Trim command, you can reduce all pixel wastage:

Figure 9-1: An image with transparency.

1. Choose Image | Trim to open the Trim dialog box.

2. In the dialog box, choose Transparent Pixels and click OK. The image is now cropped.

Optimizing and Matting

We will now prepare the graphic for the Web:

1. Open the Optimize palette and choose GIF as the format. (You would choose PNG for multiple levels of transparency or if you are exporting to Macromedia Flash.)

> **NOTE**
>
> For more information on File optimization,
> consult Chapter 5.

2. Select the Transparency box; if this box is not selected, the current background color will be used instead of a transparent background.

3. Click the Matte option (None, in this case) and choose the color closest to your web page background color, as shown in Figure 9-2. This will make the image's edges smooth on the page.

4. To use the image, choose File | Save Optimized and save it to your hard drive. Place the image in Dreamweaver as you did in Chapter 8.

Figure 9–2: Choosing a matte color.

MATTE

Notice in Figure 9-3 that the image without a matte has a jagged edge, while the matted image's edges appear much smoother. The *matte* is a thin halo of color that appears around an image's pixels, allowing it to blend smoothly into the web page if the matte's color matches the background color.

Figure 9-4 shows an image with

Figure 9–3: An image with and without a matte.

Figure 9–4: The colored matte.

a white matte placed on a black background so that you can see the white matte around the edges of the pixels. If this image were placed against a matching color background, the jagged pixels would not appear.

Animations

An *animated GIF* is a series of images that change inside the same image document. Each of these images is called a *frame*. You can vary the speed of the animation by changing the update time for individual frames. Animations are most commonly used for banners to create movement that grabs the attention of the visitor. You will create an animated banner in the next tutorial. Remember to experiment, because these principles are common to most types of animations.

> **TIP**
>
> Animations are fun to include on a web page, but beware of overusing them, because they can become annoying to viewers. Imagine a web site with 50 little animations all zooming around the page at once. Such a scene could easily give your visitors a headache or make them dizzy. Animations are powerful weapons, so use them wisely.

CREATING A SLIDING ANIMATION

For all animations, it's a good idea to create all the graphics first. In the case of a sliding animation, you will need to create the background graphic larger than the actual banner size, as shown in Figure 9-5. This will give the image some pixel space to use as it slides across the screen. You can access this banner from the book's web site (**http://www.dreamweavercafe.com/book**). The background slides across the banner and then pauses. Three boxes appear in succession; the banner will then pause for five seconds and repeat.

Figure 9–5: The background graphic.

1. In Photoshop (you can use ImageReady, but creating graphics is easier in Photoshop), create a new document at the standard banner size of 468x60 pixels.

2. Place all the graphics into layers in the banner document. Place everything at the ending position of the banner's movement, just to set up placement and make sure everything is ready, as shown in Figure 9-6.

Figure 9–6: The banner at its desired ending position.

3. Now move everything to the beginning position, as shown in Figure 9-7. Hold down the SHIFT key to constrain the movement as you slide the background across so that it stays on the same horizontal plane. Hide the layers that you want to appear later.

Figure 9–7: Beginning position.

4. Click the Edit In ImageReady button at the bottom of the toolbar to launch the document in ImageReady.

5. Open the Animation palette and the Layers palette. (You might choose to drag them together, as shown in Figure 9-8. This makes it quicker to edit the animation.)

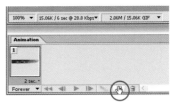

Figure 9–8: Creating a new frame.

6. Click the Duplicate Frame button in the Animation palette to create a new frame. The new frame will look identical to the first frame.

7. In the Layers palette, choose the layer that contains the background.

8. SHIFT-click and slide (while holding the SHIFT key) the background to the left in the document window. Drag the background image to the ending position for the animation, as shown in Figure 9-9.

Figure 9–9: Repositioning the graphic.

If you were to view the animation now, you would see the two frames flashing back and forth very quickly. You need to create some intermediate frames showing the image at various positions of the slide.

You could create more frames and position the image in each frame, but it's much easier to let ImageReady do all the work for you by using its Tween (in between) feature.

> **NOTE**
>
> The term *tween* is borrowed from the world of animation. Some artists, called "tween animators," create all the in-between artwork while the lead animator creates the main images that depict the movement; these are called the key animation frames (keyframes).

9. Click the Tween button in the Animation palette.

10. You will see a pop-up palette. This is the Tween palette, where you set all the Tweening options shown in Figure 9-10.

11. For the Tween With option, choose Previous Frame. This will create frames between the selected frame and the previous frame.

12. The default Frames to Add setting of 4 will work well for this instance. The more frames you add, the smoother the animation will appear, but the file size will also grow.

Figure 9–10: Tween options.

13. Click OK to apply the tween.

14. Notice that four new frames are now created. If you click the Play button in the Animation palette, you can pre-view the animation in the doc-ument window, as shown in Figure 9-11.

Figure 9–11: Testing the animation.

It's looking a lot smoother now, but the animation is still running too fast. To slow it down a bit, you'll change the delay time. You can adjust the delay on a single frame or multiple frames at once. In this instance, you will adjust multiple frames.

15. Click Frame 1 to select it. SHIFT-click the last frame. All the frames are now selected.

16. Click the little arrow (to the right of the words *0 sec*) at the bottom of any of the selected frames. You will see a pop-up menu with delay times. You can select a time from the list or choose Other to set a cus-tom delay. Choose 0.2 to set a 0.2-second delay on each frame.

Now if you now run the animation, it looks much better.

17. Select the last frame and set a 1-second delay to make the animation pause for a second at the end of the sliding movement, as in Figure 9-12.

Figure 9–12: Set a 1-second delay for the last frame.

MAKING THE BOXES APPEAR

Now let's make the boxes appear, one by one.

1. Choose the last frame and click the Duplicate Frame button.

2. In the Layers palette, click the Show/Hide eye icon to the left of the hidden layer containing the first box image (Layer 2), as shown in Figure 9-13. The image will appear in the document window.

Figure 9–13: Showing a layer.

3. Create a new frame.

4. Show the second box image.

5. Create another new frame.

6. Show the final box image; this is the end of the animation.

7. Set the delay time for the final frame to 5 seconds. The banner will now pause for five seconds before looping.

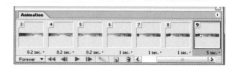

8. Test the banner again. On testing, you'll notice that the delay for each box to appear is too long and doesn't "feel" right.

9. Select frames 6 through 8 and change each of their delay times to 0.5 second.

10. Run the animation again. It should now feel right and look smooth.

11. Optimize the banner using the Optimize palette, as you would for any image. When you optimize one frame, it affects the entire animation, so you don't need to optimize each frame individually. Remember that the animation must be optimized as a GIF for it to work.

12. Choose File | Save Optimized As.

13. Save the animation as a GIF, as shown in Figure 9–14. All the frames will be saved into a single GIF file. If you open the GIF in Photoshop, you will be able to see only the first frame—this is an "ImageReady only" feature.

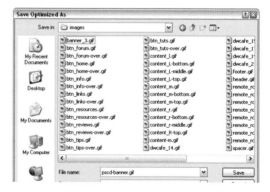

Figure 9–14: Saving the animation as a GIF.

You will insert an animation into a web page in the next tutorial.

Creating a Fading Animation and Inserting It with Dreamweaver

You have just created an animation using motion. Here you'll create a different kind of animation. This time, the animation will include some text that fades into the image from transparent. You'll create a tile ad; these are becoming more popular than banners because they are smaller and can be inserted anywhere on a web page. (Because people are so used to seeing banners, they have developed "banner blindness"—they mentally switch off and ignore banners at a subconscious level. Tile ads are newer and may be more noticeable.)

1. Open ImageReady.

2. Create a new document of 120x90 pixels, the common size for a tile ad.

3. In the New dialog box, click the Save Preset button and type in a name for the document: **tile-ad**.
This saves the settings so that they can be recalled in a single click when you create another tile ad in the future.

4. After you have saved the preset (Figure 9-15), click OK to create the new document.

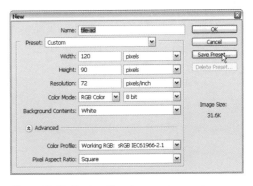

Figure 9–15: Saving the document preset.

5. Now it's time to create the graphics for the tile ad, as shown in Figure 9–16. Fade in the word *Now*. Put the item you want to fade on its own layer.

6. Hide the Now layer.

7. Create a new frame and show the Now layer. You now have a two-frame animation with the word *Now* appearing and disappearing, as shown in Figure 9–17. Let's make it smoothly fade in.

8. Click the Tween button and accept the default settings by clicking OK.

9. Set the delay time for 0.2 second and test the animation, as shown in Figure 9–18.

10. Choose a 2-second delay for the last frame. The animation will now wait for two seconds before it loops.

Figure 9–16: The layers for the new ad.

Figure 9–17: A two-frame animation.

Figure 9–18: Testing the animation.

TIP

By default, an animation will loop forever. You can choose the number of times it loops by clicking the button at the bottom left of the Animation palette and choose a number from the pop-up menu.

Adding the Animation to Your Web Page

Now you'll add the animation to your page using Dreamweaver. The animation will be placed like a normal image. You will not see any of the movement until you preview the page in your web browser.

1. Open your project's home page in Dreamweaver.

2. Click at the position where you want to insert the image. In Figure 9-19, the left-most region has been chosen.

Figure 9–19: Preparing to place the image.

3. From the Insert bar, choose the Common options and click the Image button.

4. Choose the tile-ad.gif file from the images folder and click OK, as shown in Figure 9-20.

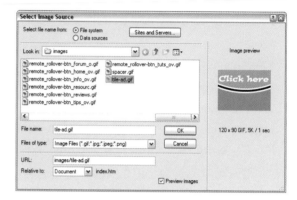

Figure 9–20: Choosing the image.

5. The image will appear on the web page as a static graphic. Click the image to select it.

6. In the Link field of the Property Inspector, type in the URL of the desired page where visitors will be redirected when they click the banner, as shown in Figure 9-21.

Figure 9–21: Adding a hyperlink.

7. Save the file and press F12 to preview it in the browser window. The animation should now be working.

CREATING ROLLOVERS IN DREAMWEAVER

As you have already discovered, it's easy to create rollovers using ImageReady. However, if you want to change a rollover or add a new one to an existing page you will run into trouble, because to generate code, you will need to output the entire HTML again and thus lose all the formatting you have done on the page in Dreamweaver. Don't fear, though, because a good solution is at hand.

> **NOTE**
>
> It's easy to create rollovers in Dreamweaver. By creating the rollovers in Dreamweaver, you won't disturb the rest of the page.

Preparing the Rollover Graphics in Photoshop

You create a rollover effect by switching out one image for another when the mouse moves over the area. You will need to prepare two images to create this effect: a normal unaffected image and another image to use for the rollover. The easiest way to do this is to create the rollover effect on a separate layer in the same document. For the sake of illustration in this tutorial, you will create a fun effect, an eye that winks when the mouse rolls over it. You can view this effect on the dreamweaverCAFE.com site. (Of course, you will probably use this technique for something more practical.)

1. Create the image you want to use for the rollover.

2. Add a new layer and create the roll-over effect, as shown in Figure 9–22.

3. Hide Layer 2 to test the effect. You should now see the normal layer and the rollover layer should be hidden, as shown in Figure 9–23.

4. You need to save two images: the regular image and another rollover image. Choose File | Save For Web. You will see the Save For Web dialog box shown in Figure 9–24.

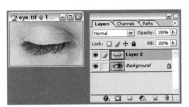

Figure 9–22: Image with the rollover layer created.

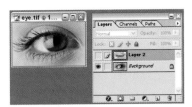

Figure 9–23: Hiding the rollover layer.

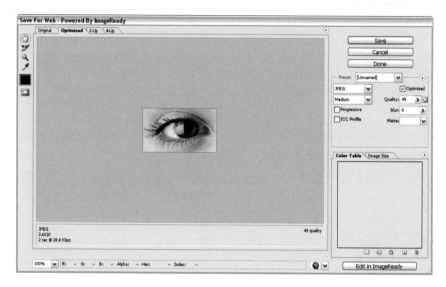

Figure 9–24: Save For Web dialog box.

> **NOTE**
>
> Save For Web is powered by ImageReady. This means that the same optimization tools are available and they work the same way they do in ImageReady, even if you don't launch ImageReady. This is a quick tool to use to export images for the Web.

5. Choose the file format (JPG in this instance), and choose the optimization settings that best suit the image. (See Chapter 5 for more information on optimization.)

6. Click Save and choose a location and name for the image. (The location should be the images folder for your web site.)

7. Now show the rollover layer (Layer 2) in the Layers palette and save the rollover image using Save For Web.

Adding a Rollover Image to Dreamweaver

You have now created the images to be used for the rollover; you can add it to your page with Dreamweaver.

1. Place the cursor inside the web page where you want to insert the image.

2. Choose the Common options from the Insert bar.

3. Select the Image drop-down and choose Rollover Image.

You will see the Insert Rollover Image dialog box, shown in Figure 9-25.

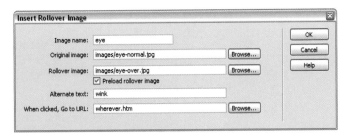

Figure 9–25: Filling out the options for the rollover image.

4. Name the image and, optionally, add some text to the Alternate Text field. (This is more commonly known as *alt* text, which will display the characters you enter as the mouse rolls over, but doesn't click, the image. The alt text will also appear on a web page if a user has turned off images in his or her browser settings.

5. In the Original Image field, click the Browse button and locate the image to be used as the normal state.

6. In the Rollover Image field, choose the image to be used as the rollover.

7. If you want the users to be directed to another page when they click the image, enter the address in the URL field.

8. Click OK and the rollover effect is added to the page.

9. Save your page and press F12 to preview it in your favorite web browser. See Figures 9-26 and 9-27 to view your eye-winking effect.

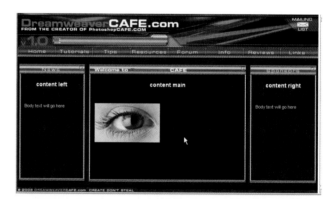

Figure 9–26: The eye is open when the cursor is placed elsewhere.

Figure 9–27: Placing your cursor on the eye closes it.

ROLLOVER EFFECTS

You can create many types of rollover effects. Here are a few ideas to spark your imagination:

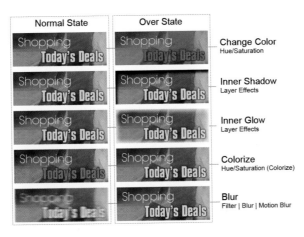

Normal State	Over State	
		Change Color Hue/Saturation
		Inner Shadow Layer Effects
		Inner Glow Layer Effects
		Colorize Hue/Saturation (Colorize)
		Blur Filter | Blur | Motion Blur

BEHAVIORS

Behaviors are scripts that can be applied to web pages without the need for any programming. Several useful behaviors ship with Dreamweaver. You can now easily create pop-up windows, drop-down menus, rollovers, and many other interface elements that were reserved for elite programmers only a few years back. One of the things that makes Dreamweaver so popular is that users can connect to Macromedia's Dreamweaver exchange site (available via **http://www.macromedia.com**) and download tons of new behaviors that extend the application's functionality. You can also connect to the exchange by clicking the Get More Behaviors link from the bottom of the program's Behaviors palette.

Creating a Rollover Using Behaviors

When you use behaviors to create rollover effects, the end results are the same as if you used the rollover feature just discussed. The difference, however, is that the behavior can be used to apply a rollover effect to an existing image, whereas the insert rollover image places a new image. Here is how it works:

1. Prepare your rollover graphic in Photoshop or ImageReady.

2. Open the Behaviors panel by choosing Window | Behaviors.

3. Choose the image to which you want to apply a rollover image, shown in Figure 9–28.

4. Click the plus sign at the top of the Behaviors panel, and choose Swap Image from the drop-down menu.

Figure 9–28: Choosing the image to which you'll apply a rollover.

5. In the Swap Image dialog box, choose the Browse button and locate the image that you want to use as the rollover. Choose the rollover image that you have prepared, as shown in Figure 9–29.

Figure 9–29: Choosing the rollover image.

6. Be sure that the Preload Images button is selected (this loads the image when the page loads so that the image appears immediately when the user rolls over because it's saved to Cache). Also make sure the Restore Images onMouseOut option is selected so that the original image will display when the mouse moves away from the image ("hot" area).

7. Click OK to apply the behavior.

8. If you look in the Behaviors panel, you will see that the Swap Image and Swap Image Restore Behaviors are now showing—these will be displayed only when the affected image is selected.

When you test the page in the browser, the rollover should now work, as shown in Figure 9-30.

Figure 9–30: Testing the rollover.

NOTE

You must preview a behavior in a browser to see its effects.

Removing a Behavior

It's very easy to remove a behavior:

1. Choose the image to which the behavior is attached.

2. Open the Behaviors panel.

3. Select the behavior that you wish to remove by clicking it.

4. Click the minus button at the top of the panel and the behavior will vanish.

CREATING DROP-DOWN (POP-UP) MENUS

Pop-up menus are menus that appear when your mouse rolls over a button. You then choose an option from those that appear. These menus are made easy by using behaviors in Dreamweaver.

The menu can be attached to any slice.

1. Choose the slice by clicking it.

2. Open the Behaviors panel.

3. Click the Plus button to add a new behavior.

4. Select Show Pop-Up Menu from the list.

5. Enter the name that you want the viewer to see in the Text field.

6. Enter the desired page URL into the Link field.

7. Press the Plus button to add another link to the menu.

8. Add the text and URL.

9. Keep adding as many links as you desire by repeating steps 7 and 8.

10. Choose the Appearance tab; this is where we will stylize the text and the color of the box.

11. Format the text by clicking the appropriate options.

12. Choose Vertical Menu if you want the menu to drop down, or Horizontal Menu for a menu that will slide out horizontally.

    There are two options with color pickers, the Up State and Over State (i.e., when the mouse moves over the area).

13. Pick a color by clicking the appropriate color picker. You can choose one of the colored squares or sample a color from the web page by clicking it, as shown in Figure 9-31.

14. Click the Advanced tab.

15. Choose the way that you want the cells to appear in this tab. The cells are the boxes behind the text. You will see a preview of the menu as you choose the options (as shown in Figure 9-32). This preview will also appear in the Appearance tab.

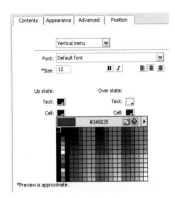

Figure 9-31: Sampling a color.

16. Click the Position tab to choose the way the menus will appear.

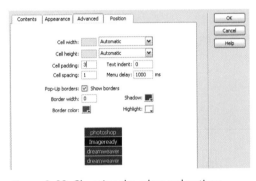

Figure 9-32: Choosing the advanced options.

17. Select the desired position. The menu will appear in the position of the blue line on the chosen button.

18. Figure 9-33 shows the working menu as it is previewed in a web browser.

Figure 9–33: A drop-down menu in action.

Making Multitiered Menus

In this section, we'll create a multitiered menu, which is a menu within a menu. An example of this is when you choose a drop-down menu and see an arrow on an option. When you roll over the option, another menu will appear.

> **TIP**
>
> To modify a pop-up menu, double-click Show Pop-Up Menu from the Behaviors panel.

1. Choose any of the menu items by clicking them on the Contents tab of the Pop-Up Menu dialog box. You can also create a new menu item in the same fashion as we have just done in the previous steps.

2. Click the Indent Menu button to move the menu to a submenu of the previous option.

3. You can click the up or down arrows to move the option up or down in the menu.

Figure 9–34 shows a submenu in use.

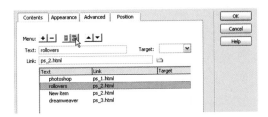

Figure 9–34: Previewing the submenu.

PART IV

MOVE BEYOND YOUR LOCAL COMPUTER

CHAPTER 10

CREATE FORMS AND E-COMMERCE CAPABILITIES

This chapter focuses on forms and how to create them using Dreamweaver. Forms are a great way to get feedback from your visitors. Working forms consist of various objects that we will be using. At the end of the chapter, you will generate a form from PayPal and insert it in your web page to provide a way for online shoppers to pay for merchandise.

FORMS

Here we'll walk through setting up a form and using the objects. You will need to contact your web host to finalize the form and connect it to the Internet; with so many connection and posting options available (as you'll learn about it a bit), you must determine what methods are supported by your host before you can "go live" with your site on their servers.

Choose the Forms option from the Insert bar, and you'll see icons that you can use to insert various objects onto your page. Each of these objects perform a task that allows your visitors to communicate. Figure 10-1 shows the Insert bar and the Forms options.

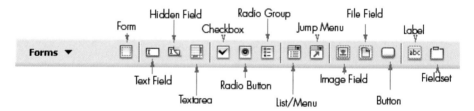

Figure 10-1: The Forms Insert bar.

- **Form:** Defines a form region; everything inside this region will be part of the form

- **Text Field:** Allows the user to input text

- **Hidden Field:** Allows the form to pass certain information to the server

- **Textarea:** Allows the user to input paragraphs of text

- **Checkbox:** Displays a user preference for an option with a checkbox

- **Radio Button:** Displays a user preference for an option with a radio button

- **Radio Group:** Creates a group of radio buttons

- **List/Menu:** Creates a scrolling menu so the user can select a option or multiple options
- **Jump Menu:** Creates a menu that offers a hyperlink when an option is selected (We will create one in Chapter 11.)
- **Image Field:** Uses an image as a button in a form
- **File Field:** Adds a button that allows the user to attach a file from a computer
- **Button:** Allows the user to submit and reset forms, but other actions may be applied to buttons as well
- **Label:** Allows you to add label text to the form
- **Fieldset:** Draws a box around the contained text

Creating a Form

First, you need to define your form:

1. Place the cursor on the page and click the Form button. A box outlined in red dashes will be displayed on the page, as shown next. This box defines the content area of your form. All the form items must be contained within this area or they will not work properly.

2. Now you'll create a table to help you organize the form. Place the cursor inside the Form area that we just defined.

3. Click the Insert Table button, choose Insert | Table, or press CTRL-ALT-T (OPTION-CMD-T on the Mac).

4. In the Table dialog box, shown in Figure 10-2, type **2** in the Columns field and type in the number of rows you'll need to accommodate each of the options you want to appear in your form. In this case, type in **5**.

5. Select a header style for the form.

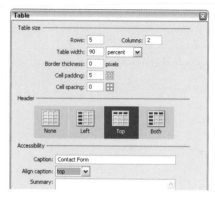

Figure 10–2: Creating a table.

> **TIP**
>
> Use the Accessibility options (Header and Caption) in the dialog box to make the form readable and accessible to users with disabilities.

6. Click OK to create the table.

7. Enter the text for the form and format it manually or by using (CSS). Figure 10-3 shows the form's layout.

8. Place the mouse in the table cell to the right of the Name text.

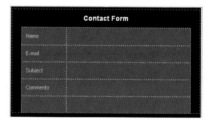

Figure 10–3: The table in a form, ready for some input objects.

9. Click the Text Field button.

10. A white box that represents the input field will appear. Users can enter alphanumeric or password text here.

11. In the Property Inspector, name the field in the TextField field, as shown in Figure 10-4, to identify the field in the form. The other options in the Property Inspector, such as Max Chars, are useful to accommodate user input of phone numbers and credit card numbers;

you can limit the amount of characters that can be entered into a field. Create a text field for each piece of information you want to collect.

Figure 10–4: Naming the field in the Property Inspector.

12. Now create a place where the user can input more than a single line of text. You will create a box that will scroll as it is filled with text. Click the Textarea button. The text area is shown in the web page in Figure 10-5.

Figure 10–5: The form so far.

13. Select the Comments area and set the options in the Property Inspector, as shown in Figure 10-6. Type **8** in the Num Lines field to display eight lines of text. In the field, after the eight lines of text, a scroll bar will appear; the user can add more lines of comments by scrolling.

Figure 10–6: Setting options in the Property Inspector.

Notice in Figure 10-7 that the Comments area has now increased to accommodate the new settings.

CREATING A LIST/MENU

Now you'll use the List/Menu button to add a drop-down menu with multiple options available for the user to choose. A *list* will allow the user to choose more than one option.

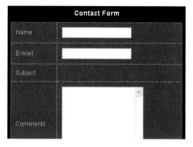

Figure 10–7: The form with an expanded Comments area.

1. Place the mouse insertion point in the page.

2. Click the List/Menu button.

3. Now set the options for the drop-down menu. Click the List Values Button in the Property Inspector.

4. The List Values dialog will appear. Enter the Label (what the user will see) in the left field. Enter the Value (what the form will identify the field as) in the right field.

5. To add the next option, click the Plus button, as shown here.

6. Enter the other options, as shown next. Note that you can press the TAB key to jump to a new line

rather than clicking the Plus button. You can reposition the placement of any item by selecting it and clicking the up and down arrows on the top right.

7. Click OK to add the menu to the page.

8. Press F12 to test the menu in a web browser.

   Users can now click the drop-down menu and select a single option, as shown in Figure 10-8.

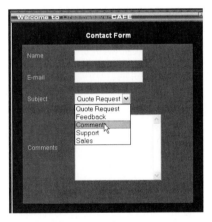

Figure 10–8: Testing the menu.

ALLOWING USERS TO SELECT MULTIPLE OPTIONS

At times, you may want the user to be able to select more than one option; in such cases, use a list.

1. Select the menu you just created.

2. In the Properties Inspector, click the List radio button.

3. Choose the Selections Allow Multiple checkbox, and then choose the field you want to appear on the menu when the user first sees it, as shown in Figure 10-9.

Figure 10–9: Setting the properties of the list.

Creating Buttons

The user will need a way to send the form to you after it's filled out. We will enable this by adding a Submit button:

1. Choose a place to insert the button by clicking with your mouse in the web page.

2. Click the Insert button.

3. A button will now appear on the page as a Submit button, with the default label and action.

CREATING A RESET BUTTON

Now you need to create a Reset button that will let the user erase all the contents of the form—this is a like a "start again" button.

1. Create a Submit button as you did in the last procedure. Figure 10–10 shows the page with two Submit buttons created. Now you'll change one of them to a Reset button.

2. Select the button by clicking it.

Figure 10–10: Two buttons on the page.

3. In the Properties Inspector, change the Action to Reset Form, as shown in Figure 10-11.

Figure 10–11: Changing the action of a button.

4. Press F12 to test the page in a web browser. Fill out the fields with some text and click the Reset button, shown in Figure 10-12. The Reset button should now work. The Submit button will not work yet.

Figure 10–12: Testing the button in a web browser.

Creating a Checkbox

Sometimes you will want to supply a way for the user to check an option. This is a common feature for a mailing list form—when the user checks the box, you know that he or she is happy to receive mailings from you. It's a good idea to make the box initially checked so that the visitor can uncheck the box if he or she does *not* want to receive mailings (you will get more people to sign up for your mailing list this way).

> **NOTE**
>
> Anti-spam legislation in some regions requires that you obtain permission before adding someone to your mailing list. But even without this legislation, it's good business practice to get permission before mailing information so you don't upset customers.

1. Insert the cursor on the page where you want the checkbox to appear.

2. Click the Checkbox button.

3. In the page, enter some text next to the button to identify it for the user.

4. In the Property Inspector, enter a value in the CheckBox Name field, as shown in Figure 10–13.

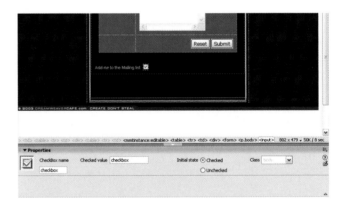

Figure 10–13: Setting the properties for the page.

5. In the Initial State area, select the Checked radio button.

6. Save the page and test the button in a web browser.

Making the Form Work

You may have noticed by now that when you click the Submit button, nothing happens. That is because the form has to be told what to do. Now it's time to make the buttons on your form perform one of two main actions: submit the information to a database where it is stored or e-mail the information to someone. The second method is most common, although forms can be processed in many ways. Often, form mail script is used, which resides on the web server. The script indicates what should happen with the form information and how it should be processed: Cold Fusion is a scripting language that works with databases to process information; Active Server Pages (ASP) is a Microsoft technology used to process information; and Hypertext Preprocessor (PHP) is an open-source scripting language used to process information. As mentioned earlier, before you post your site on the Web, you need to check with your web host to determine which type of processing is best to use on its servers. Most web hosts provide all the documentation you need to connect your form to the Internet, and some hosts will provide the service for you at a nominal fee.

Before you submit your site to your web host, you need to modify the forms and enter the appropriate parameters. One place where you can enter the parameters is in the Property Inspector.

1. Choose <form> from the tag selector at the bottom of the document window, as shown in Figure 10-14. The available options will appear

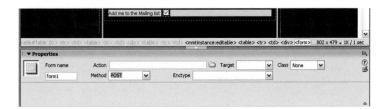

Figure 10–14: The submit properties.

241

in the Property Inspector. Enter the address of the script into the Action field and choose POST as the Method.

2. Look at the page in code view (Figure 10-15), and you will notice a line of code (fourth line from the top) that has <form name=, method=, and action=>. You can enter the script's URL address directly into the code if you prefer using code view over design view.

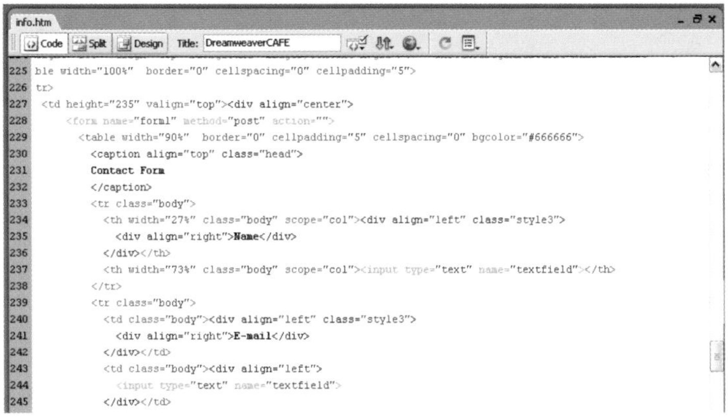

Figure 10–15: The HTML for the form.

3. Once you've configured the script, enter the script's URL address into the Action field in the Property Inspector, and it will work.

4. Create two normal HTML pages: name them Thankyou.htm and sorry.htm. Obviously, in the Thankyou.htm page, type in information thanking the user for entering his or her information and perhaps offering more information or links to sites. The sorry.htm page will tell the user that he or she has improperly filled out the form and indicate which fields still need to be included. The user will be directed to one of these pages, depending on whether or not the form submission was successful.

5. The instructions for directing the users (called *Redirect*) to these pages will be with the instructions for setting up the script from your web host. (You will learn about web hosts in Chapter 12.)

CREATE A JUMP MENU

A *jump menu* is a drop-down menu that offers hyperlinks to other sites or pages, a great way to create a list of links that takes up very little space on your site. When the user selects an option on the list, he or she is redirected to another web page either on the same site or a different site. Here's how it's done:

1. Open the page to which you want to attach the jump menu.

2. Click in the location where you want the menu to appear.

3. Click the Jump Menu button.

4. In the Insert Jump Menu dialog box shown in Figure 10-16, type in the text that will be displayed in the Text field.

5. Enter the URL into the When Selected, Go To URL field. Optionally, choose which window the page will appear in.

6. Select the Insert Go Button After Menu option, as shown in Figure 10-16, if you want a Go button to appear on the page. This allows the user to go to the currently selected item by clicking

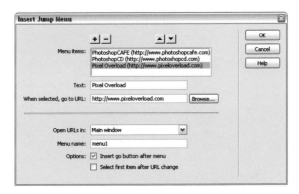

Figure 10–16: Setting the properties of the jump menu.

this button (otherwise, the user will be taken to the new page by choosing the option in the menu).

7. Click the Plus button at the top of the dialog box to enter another menu item.

8. Keep adding items until you are satisfied, as shown in Figure 10-16.

9. Click OK to add the menus to the page.

10. Press F12 to test is the jump menu in the browser, as shown in Figure 10-17.

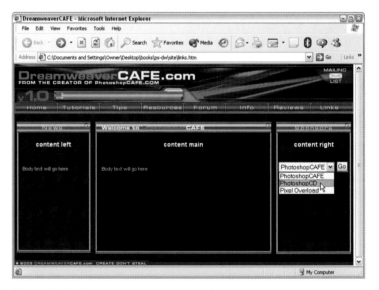

Figure 10–17: Testing the menu on the web page.

When a user chooses a site from the drop-down menu, the page will jump to the new site, shown in Figure 10-18.

Figure 10–18: Jump to a new page.

E-COMMERCE

E-commerce is modern jargon for "doing business on the Internet." What makes e-commerce work is the ability for shoppers to buy items online and the ability for a business to receive payment for goods or services via the Internet. Generally speaking, this involves a shopping cart (a way for shoppers to store selected purchases) and a merchant account (a way for businesses to store payment information and collect money). You can add e-commerce to your web site without hassle by using PayPal, an online service that processes payments for you. The PayPal service takes a small percentage (approximately five percent at the time of this writing) of the transaction as a fee for the service. This is a good option to use when you are starting out or making small transactions.

Let's walk through the process of adding PayPal to a web page. When your business grows and you are generating substantial business, you can switch from PayPal and invest in a shopping cart and merchant account.

Signing Up for a PayPal Account

Before you can use PayPal to receive payments, you need to set up an account.

1. Log onto **http://paypal.com**, the PayPal home page shown in Figure 10-19.

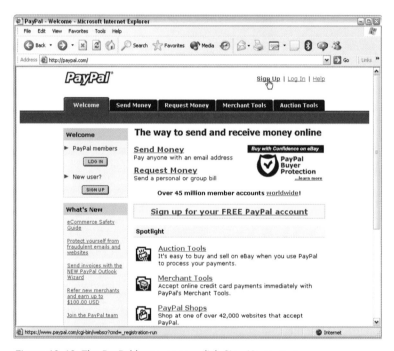

Figure 10–19: The PayPal home page—click Sign Up to start.

2. Click Sign Up if you don't yet have an account.

3. Choose the kind of account you would like to set up: Personal Account or Business Account, as shown in Figure 10-20. Choose Business Account, and then click Continue.

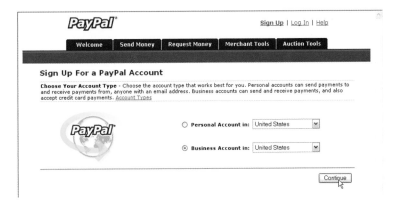

Figure 10–20: Choose an account type.

4. PayPal makes it easy to fill out the forms completely, like the one shown in Figure 10-21.

Figure 10–21: Fill out the questionnaire.

5. Part of the sign-up process requires your bank account information. Follow the onscreen prompts. You will then verify the account by accepting to pay a small deposit. (The money will be taken out of your account first—it's less than a dollar at the moment.) Once the verification is completed, you will be ready to use the service.

Creating a Buy Now Button

When you have signed up for your merchant account at PayPal, you are ready to add a Buy Now button to your site so that people can pay you for your products and services.

1. Log onto PayPal using your user name (e-mail address) and password, as shown in Figure 10-22.

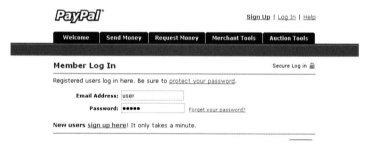

Figure 10–22: Logging onto PayPal.

> **CAUTION**
>
> Never share your password with anyone—not even someone posing as a PayPal employee.

The Overview page appears with pertinent information, as shown in Figure 10-23 (I have blanked out a few lines of personal information). Notice that Verified appears as the Status and a number of satisfied transactions are listed. The Verified status shows that the business has conducted itself well and offers comfort and security to the shopper.

Figure 10–23: The Overview page.

2. Click the Merchant Tools tab at the top of the page. As shown in Figure 10-24, you can create a shopping cart (for multiple products)

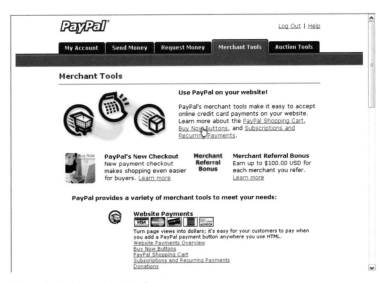

Figure 10–24: Merchant Tools page.

and set up subscriptions and recurring payments here. Now you'll set up a Buy Now button to sell a single product.

3. Click the Buy Now Buttons link.

4. You'll be directed to a page that explains the button and services in detail. When you have read the areas of interest (recommended) and are ready to create the button, click the Get Started! link, as shown in Figure 10-25.

Figure 10–25: Click Get Started!

5. Fill out the form completely, as shown in Figure 10-26. Enter the item and price.

6. You can also choose to create a custom button if you wish. You will need to create the button and upload it to the Internet. Then you link its location in the Button Image URL field in the middle of the screen. For now, use the standard Buy Now button supplied on this form.

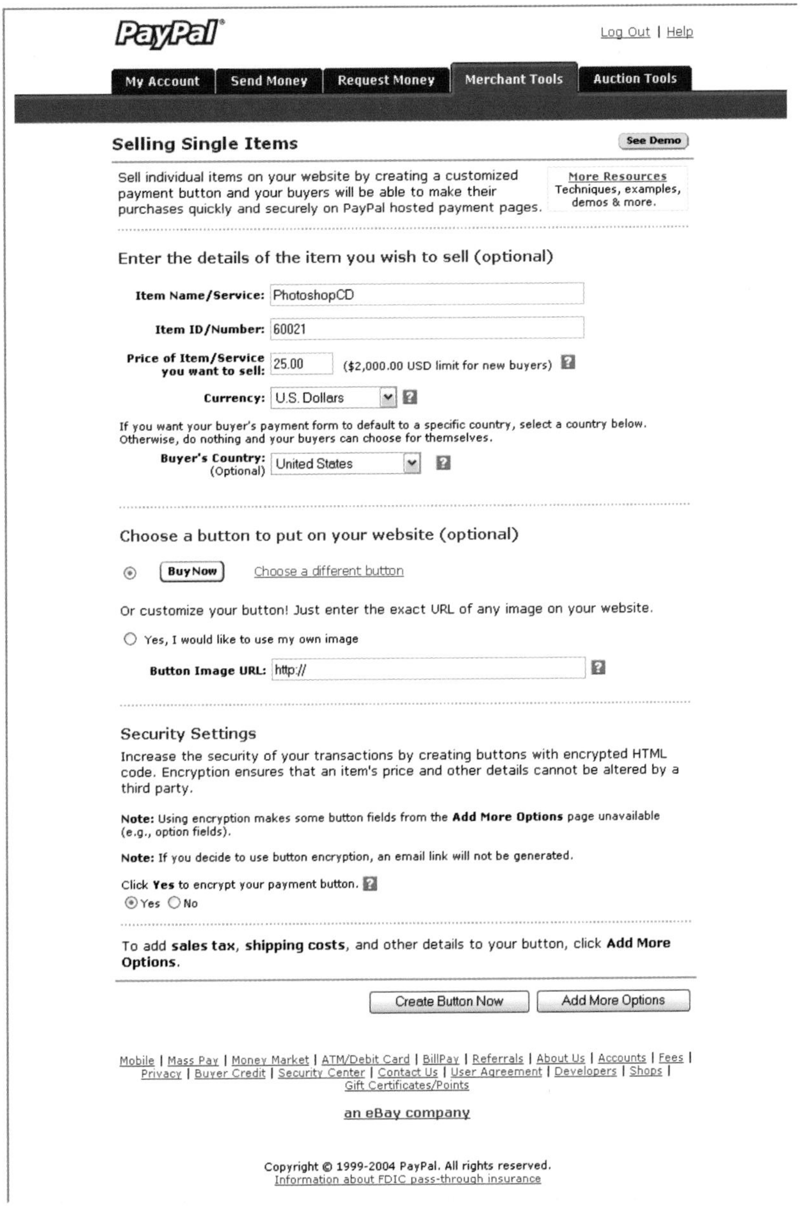

Figure 10–26: Entering your data.

7. When you are ready, click the Create Button Now button.

8. You will see a page with a window that contains HTML code to add to your web page. Click inside the text box and press CTRL-A (CMD-A on the Mac) to select all the text, as shown in Figure 10-27.

Add a button to your website

Copy your custom HTML code
Copy the code below just like you would normal text.

Note: If you are using button encryption, an email link will not be generated. To turn button encryption off and create an email link, click your browser's **Back** button, click the No radio butt turn off button encryption, and then click **Create Button Now**.

Encrypted HTML code
for Websites:
(Copy and paste this
HTML code onto your
website)

```
<form
action="https://www.paypal.com/cgi
-bin/webscr" method="post">
<input type="hidden" name="cmd"
value="_s-xclick">
<input type="image"
```

Figure 10–27: Selecting the code.

9. Press CTRL-C (CMD-C on Mac) to copy the text to the clipboard.

10. Open Dreamweaver and click where you want the button to appear on your page.

11. In Code view or Split view, find the insertion point location, as

```
238  align="top" background="images/content-m.gif"><!-- InstanceBeginEditable name="middle" -->
239  0%"  border="0" cellspacing="0" cellpadding="5">
240
241  235" valign="top"><div align="center">
242  ="head">content main</p>
243  ="body">|</p>
244
245
```

Figure 10–28: The insertion point in HTML in Dreamweaver.

shown in Figure 10-28 (look for the I-beam). Click the insertion point inside the code pane to make Code view active.

12. Paste the code into the code window (press CTRL-V, or CMD-V on the Mac), as shown in Figure 10-29.

```
241              <td height="235" valign="top"><div align="center">
242                  <p class="head">content main</p>
243                  <p class="body"><form action="https://www.paypal.com/cgi-bin/webscr" method="post">
244  type="hidden" name="cmd" value="_s-xclick">
245  type="image" src="https://www.paypal.com/en_US/i/btn/x-click-but23.gif" border="0" name="submit" alt="Make p
246  type="hidden" name="encrypted" value="-----BEGIN PKCS7-----MIIHLwYJKoZIhvcNAQcEoIIHIDCCBxwCAQExggEwMIIBLAIBA
     1MDIxMzEwMTMxNVowgY4xCzAJBgNVBAYTAlVTMQswCQYDVQQIEwJDQTEWMBQGA1UEBxMNTW91bnRhaW4gVmlldzEUMBIGA1UEChMLUGF5UGF
     WluIFZpZpZXcxFDASBgNVBAoTC1BheVBhbCBJbmMuMRMwEQYDVQQLFApsaXZ1X2N1cnRzMREwDwYDVQQDFAhsaXZ1X2FwaTEcMBoGCSqGSIb3D
```

Figure 10–29: The pasted code in Dreamweaver.

13. If you view your page in Design view, you will see that the form has been added along with the hidden form elements. The yellow shields with *H's* on them indicate hidden fields.

14. Enter your product information and price as text in the form, as shown in Figure 10-30. You could also use an image of the product to attract more attention and offer more information.

Figure 10–30: Enter product information.

15. Press F12 to test your addition in a browser. The Buy Now button, shown next, should work and actually connect you to the PayPal site, where users can submit credit card information.

Figure 10-31 shows a working page that uses the PayPal Buy Now button. This is my page, where I sell Photoshop training video CDs. Notice that I have created a custom Buy Now button. I've also added more information to the page, such as product descriptions, which is a good idea.

Figure 10–31: Custom button on a working web page.

When the viewer clicks the Buy Now button, he or she jumps to a PayPal page that shows the amount of the purchase as well as the shipping price. (You set up all this information in your PayPal business account.) Figure 10–32 shows the PhotoshopCAFE Store order page.

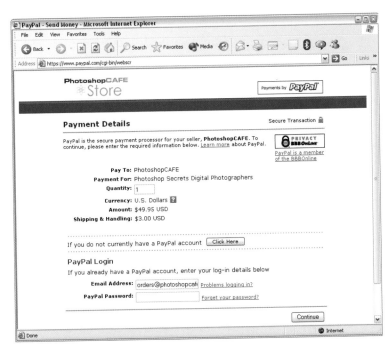

Figure 10–32: Product order page.

The visitor can then enter an e-mail address and password to log into PayPal, where he or she can enter credit card information. Because the merchant (you and me) never sees the credit card numbers, this offers the shopper more security. PayPal is careful that only legitimate businesses use its services, so you know that your purchase is safe and legitimate.

The great thing about using PayPal is that you can begin selling products right away (as soon as your account is verified) and no monthly fees are tacked on. The only fees PayPal charges are for transactions.

> **NOTE**
>
> You can also use PayPal to send and receive money to or from friends and clients; you will incur the standard fee for this. Simply transfer the money from PayPal to your bank account when you want to take possession of the funds in your PayPal account. This is a free transaction and takes about three days to complete.

CHAPTER 11

ADDING THE COOL FACTOR

This chapter might be the most fun chapter in the book; you will learn some cool tricks that make people look at your web page and ask, "How did they do that?" Here we go beyond the working project to explore oft-used techniques such as inline frames, jump menus, pop-up windows, and more, to add a bit of zip to your web pages.

USING FRAMES TO CREATE AN IMAGE GALLERY

Frames let you display multiple pages within a single window. While each of these pages is independent from the others, each can be controlled from within other frames. Here we will build a gallery to showcase the "Snooki" characters developed by my friend Ali Sabet. We'll create a frame on the left side of the window that will contain thumbnail images and act as a navigation aid. When you click a thumbnail on the left, the frame on the right will display the full-sized image. The frame on the left will remain unchanged.

An HTML page acts as a base page on which other pages will be loaded. For example, the following illustration shows a page called main.htm that is split into two regions called *frames*. (You can divide a page into as many frames as you wish.) These frames themselves contain no viewable content; they are, in fact, areas where other HTML pages will be loaded and will appear. Each of these frames has a frame name. The left frame is named leftFrame and the right frame is named mainFrame. We choose initial pages that will be loaded into each of these frames by default. The file one.htm will appear in leftFrame and two.htm will appear in mainFrame. These three documents—the base HTML page plus the two frame documents—are called the *frameset*.

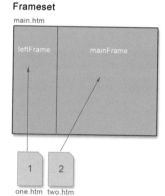

By using the frame names as *targets*, you can control into which frame the new pages will be loaded. Although this sounds complicated, it's not so difficult to achieve using Dreamweaver:

1. Create a new HTML page in Dreamweaver, as you did earlier in the book.

2. Choose File | New | Basic Page | HTML, or just choose New HTML from the Startup screen.

3. Choose the Layout option from the Insert bar.

4. Click the Insert Frame drop-down and choose a frame layout.

5. Resize the frames by clicking and dragging on the divider bar, as shown in Figure 11-1.

Figure 11–1: Resizing the frames.

> **NOTE**
>
> Once saved, the frames can be resized only from the host HTML page. Look for the cols tag in the code view and enter the width in pixels.

6. Choose File | Save All. You will save the host frame first; I named it snookie_2.htm.

7. Click Save and another window will prompt you to save the first HTML page. I named it nav.htm. Click Save.

8. Next, you are prompted to save the next page, which I called main_1.htm. You have now saved and named all the pages for the frameset.

You can now add some content to the left frame. (I have inserted the thumbnail images that I created in a previous tutorial.)

> **NOTE**
>
> To select a frame, click inside its window. The tab on the top of the window will display the title of the HTML page that is inserted into the frame. (On the Mac, the name will appear in the title bar.) Figure 11-2 shows the right frame selected and main_1.htm displayed in the tab.

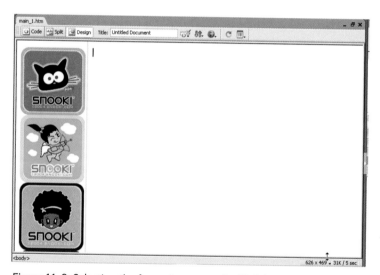

Figure 11–2: Selecting the frame (Image credit: Ali Sabet www.sabet.com).

9. Add the content for the first page. In Figure 11-3, I added the full-sized image for the first thumbnail.

Figure 11–3: Adding content into the main frame window.

Setting Frame Properties

Now let's set properties for the frames:

1. Choose Window | Frames.

The frame names will appear in the Frames panel. Note that these names are not the same names used for the HTML pages that are loaded into the frames.

2. Click a frame in the panel to select the frame, and its properties will appear in the Property Inspector. In Figure 11-4, mainFrame is select-

Figure 11–4: Frame properties.

ed and its name is displayed in the Frame Name field of the Property Inspector. You can also see the name of the HTML page that populates that frame—main_1.htm.

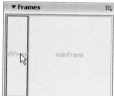

3. In the Frames panel, click the left frame.

   You'll see the nav.htm page loading into the leftFrame frame.

4. Because several image thumbnails appear in the left frame, they cannot all be displayed at once. This means that the viewer will need to scroll down the window to see all the images. In the Property Inspector, set Scroll to Auto, as shown in Figure 11-5.

Figure 11–5: Setting the Scroll property to Auto.

Creating Pages to Load into the Frame

When you click an image thumbnail in the left frame, the image will be loaded into the right frame. To make this happen, we'll create a new HTML page for each of the full-sized images.

1. Create a basic HTML page and place an image on it. Save this page with a meaningful name.

2. Create a basic HTML page for each of the images. Figure 11-6 shows all the pages created.

Figure 11–6: The HTML pages.

TARGETING THE FRAME WINDOWS

Now let's make the HTML pages open in the right frame when you click a thumbnail on the left frame.

1. Select the first thumbnail image by clicking it.

2. Click the folder icon to the right of the Link field in the Property Inspector.

3. In the Select File dialog box, choose the page you want to open when the thumbnail is clicked, as shown in Figure 11-7.

Figure 11–7: Selecting the linked page.

4. To make the new page open in the right frame, in the Property Inspector, choose mainFrame from the drop-down list in the Target field, as shown here:

You have just targeted pishi.htm to open in the main frame of snooki-2.htm.

5. Select each of the image thumbnails, as shown in Figure 11-8, and assign a page and target to each of the links.

6. Finally, test the frameset in a browser by pressing F12. Scroll down the left frame and click each of the thumbnails—watch the main image change each time you click a thumbnail, as shown in Figure 11-9.

Figure 11-8: Adding links to the thumbnails.

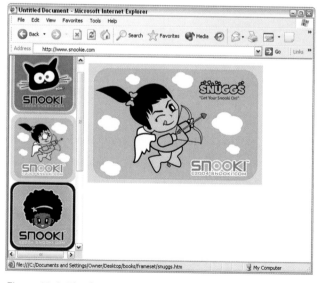

Figure 11-9: The frames in a web browser.

> **NOTE**
>
> When you link to the frameset from another page, you will want to link to the page that controls the frames. The HTML pages that populate the frameset will be loaded by the control page.

Considerations in Using Frames

Although frames are useful, they do have some drawbacks:

- Not all browsers support frames, although most current browsers do so.

- Because each page can be accessed outside a frameset by search engines, sites built in frames do not always appear when using search engines. The viewer can enter a page without the frames for navigation.

- Because you can open a new page in a frame, if that page also contains a frame, you can potentially have many frames within frames and get lost in "frame hell."

Even considering these drawbacks, frames definitely have their place on web pages, and if they are used tastefully, they can be great assets to a site. Picture galleries, discussed next, are ideal situations that lend themselves well to using frames.

CREATING A PICTURE GALLERY USING PHOTOSHOP'S AUTOMATION TOOLS

Now consider what you have learned so far in this chapter, and let Photoshop create the gallery for you automatically. (So why did we just create it manually? Because you now understand frames and are able to adapt them for many situations.) Photoshop makes it easy to build an online picture gallery in just a few steps from the file browser:

1. Launch the file browser and navigate to the folder of images that you want to include in your gallery.

> **TIP**
>
> If Photoshop's palettes are covering up the File Browser, you can hide them temporarily by pressing the TAB key. Press it again to bring back the palettes.

2. Click an image and open the Metadata tab, shown in Figure 11-10. A lot of information can be stored here, such as image information, camera settings at time of capture, and even the location when the photo was taken, if your camera is equipped with a global positioning system (GPS). Under the IPTC section of the Metadata tab, notice that a pencil icon appears in the left column of some fields, which means that these fields are editable. Enter a description—this will appear as a caption on your web page. Enter the Author and Copyright information for the image.

Figure 11–10: Adding a description.

NOTE

To create more fields, right-click (CONTROL-click on Mac) a thumbnail and choose File Info.

3. Click the check mark at the bottom of the window to apply the custom fields to the image. This information will now be attached to the image and travel with the image wherever it goes.

4. Let's move on to the gallery. In the file browser, CTRL-click (CMD-click) each of the images you want to include in the gallery. You don't have to open the images in Photoshop.

5. Choose Automate | Web Photo Gallery from the file browser's menu.

6. Select a style for the gallery; you can see a preview to the right, as shown in Figure 11-11. Note that some options will not be available with certain styles.

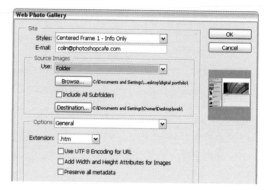

7. Enter your e-mail address so that visitors can contact you.

Figure 11–11: Choosing options for the web photo gallery.

8. In the Source Images section, you will choose the images and decide where you will save the gallery. In the Use field, select Folder from the drop-down list to use an entire folder of images, or choose Selected Images From File Browser. Choose this option to use the images you selected in step 4.

9. Click the Destination button and either create or select the folder where you'll save the gallery.

Setting the Options

In the Web Photo Gallery dialog box, under Options, you'll see a drop-down menu. Let's look at the most important items here; the others can remain at default settings.

From the Options drop-down menu, choose Banner. Here you will enter the title of the gallery and personal information.

Choose Large Images from the drop-down menu, and you can set sizing information for your images' display. You can choose the default or increase the size if you wish.

Notice the File Size slider, which sets the JPG compression. The further left the slider, the faster the images will load, but they will be lower in quality and suffer from JPEG artifacts (pixellated blocks and smudged details). Move the slider to the right and the quality will be much better, but it will take longer for the image to download. The setting you use depends on your intended audience. If viewers are using fast connections, such as cable or DSL, use a higher setting. If they are using dial-up modems or are located overseas, use lower settings. If you are unsure, a setting of 5 will produce a healthy compromise.

The Security setting allows you to *watermark* your images to make it difficult for people to "borrow" them and use them without paying you the proper fee or credit (one of the biggest fears of photographers and designers desiring to post images online).

> **TIP**
>
> Convert your logo to a font, and you can select it as the watermark. You can use software such as Macromedia Fontographer to perform this logo-to-font conversion. Other programs are also available, such as Scanfont from Fontlab and The Font Creator Program from Brothersoft.

Here's how to add a watermark to images:

1. Under Custom Text, type in a message that you want to use for a watermark. In the following, the copyright symbol is used.

2. Choose the font, size, color, opacity, and position of the watermark. The Opacity setting determines the strength of the watermark. I prefer to use white and set the opacity at 38 percent; this allows the watermark to protect the image without covering too much. Notice that the copyright watermark can be clearly seen in Figure 11-12.

When you are happy with all the Option settings, slick OK. Photoshop will now do all the work for you. Sit back and relax while you are being saved hours of work. You don't even have to resize any of your images first. All the thumbnails, HTML, and Java script will be built for you.

When Photoshop has finished, it will launch your new gallery in your web browser, as shown in Figure 11-12. You can scroll through the thumbnails and click any of them to display the full-sized images.

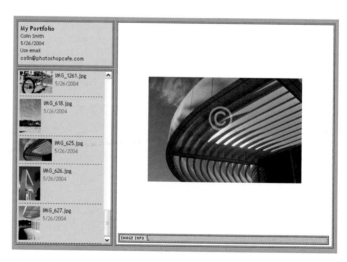

Figure 11-12: Viewing the final gallery.

CREATING INLINE FRAMES (IFRAMES)

Instead of dividing the page into several pages, an inline frame can be loaded into an existing page. This iframe will scroll within the host page without the user having to scroll the host page itself. This is an excellent way to load scrolling content into a web page. The iframe will scroll within a HTML page, as shown here.

Figure 11-13 shows a web page that uses iframes.

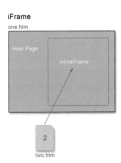

Figure 11–13: A web page that is using iframes.

Iframes are easy to create—so easy, in fact, that it's a snap to hand-code them. Iframes are attached to an existing host page and consist of four parts:

- **Host page:** The HTML page in which the iframe is loaded
- **Target page:** The page that will be loaded into the host page (`src="ourPage.htm"`)
- **Size:** The size in pixels (`Width="200" Height="200"`)
- **Properties:** The name for the frame, the border size, and scrolling options

Let's create an iframe:

1. Begin with two HTML documents: the host page to which you will add the code and the target page that will be loaded into the host page. In Dreamweaver, choose Split view to view both documents.

2. In the host page, choose the location for the iframe (it must be between the <body> tags.

3. Type the code to create the iframe:

   ```
   <iframe>
   ```

   The codes in HTML must be closed with a slash (/) character, like so: `</iframe>`, so the line will look like this before you add content:

   ```
   <iframe></iframe>
   ```

4. Target the page that will load into the frame using the scr= command:

   ```
   <iframe scr="newPage.htm"></iframe>
   ```

5. Now choose sizes for the iframe. Choose a height and width in pixels and add it to the code:

   ```
   <iframe src="newPage.htm" width="200" height="200"></iframe>
   ```

Your code should look something like this when you're done.

6. Test the page by previewing it in the browser.

The target page should now load into the host page, as shown in Figure 11-14. (If it doesn't, make sure that the name is correct and that both pages are in the same directory.) That's pretty neat. You may want to experiment with the sizes by changing their values for height and width.

Figure 11–14: The page in the web browser showing the iframe loaded.

7. Now let's get rid of the border around the iframe. You can make it invisible by adding this code:

```
<iframe src="newPage.htm" width="200" height="200"
frameborder="0"></iframe>
```

The frame border should now be hidden.

This is where all the content will go. Say all the words that you want to say and add pictures right here on this page. This is new page.htm loaded into the iframe.

We will now repeat this text so that you can see how it scrolls.

Loading New Pages into the Iframe

What if you want to load another page into the iframe? If you add a link and click it, the new page will take over the whole window instead of appearing in the iframe. You need to target the iframe for the new page. To do this, you must first provide a name for the frame. You name iframes in the same way that you name traditional frames.

1. Open the iframe host page in Dreamweaver. Add name= code to name the frame and to allow other pages to load into it. Let's call the frame *fr*. When you load a new page now, *fr* will be chosen as the target frame. The complete code should look something like this:

```
<iframe src="new page.htm" width="200" height="200"
frameborder="0" name="fr"></iframe>
```

2. Add some links for people to click. In this example, text links are used, but you can use buttons or another object if you prefer.

3. Highlight Link2, as shown in Figure 11-15 (number 1 in the figure).

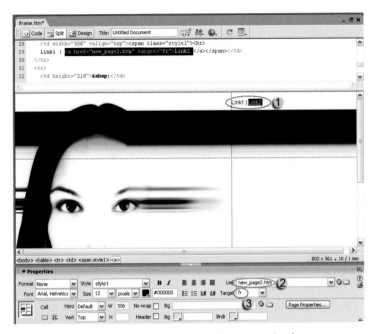

Figure 11–15: Setting the options to load the page in the iframe.

4. Link to the new page in the Property Inspector (2). This will load the new page when the button is clicked.

5. Add the frame name *fr* in the Target field (3). The page will now receive an order to load in the frame named fr, which just happens to be our iframe.

Notice that two links are included in Figure 11-15 (1). This provides a way for the user to go back to the original page (new page.htm) in the iframe after it has been replaced by our new page.

Figure 11–16: Setting the link to load the original page.

6. Highlight Link1 and add the code shown in Figure 11–16.

Figure 11–17: The iframe in action in the web browser.

7. Now test the page in a web browser, as shown in Figure 11-17. Click Link2 and the new page will open in the iframe. Click Link1 and the original page will load back up.

CREATING POP-UP WINDOWS

Before we explore the techniques involved in creating pop-up windows, let me begin with a word of warning. Because this technology has been so abused by junk advertising, pop-ups have a bad rap. For example, while using the Internet, you click a link to open a page and 20 pop-up windows appear. If you are like me, you quickly close all the windows and go to another site. Some viewers employ pop-up blocking software, which disables the windows from opening.

Not all pop-up windows are evil, however. You may want to launch your page without all the toolbars, have extra information appear such as a larger version of an image or more information on a product, or need to advertise a product or service on your site.

> **TIP**
>
> I am not advocating pop-up advertising and recommend you keep it to a minimum, because it infuriates some visitors.

Pop-up windows need something to trigger them—usually it is a link. You can attach pop-up windows to existing links and buttons and cause the windows to pop up when another link is clicked. In this example, we are going to attach a pop-up window to an image map on an image. The process is the same no matter which method you choose. If you are attaching to a slice or button, skip ahead to step 4. In our example, the pop-up will launch when the user clicks the Clik Here (misspelling intentional) area.

1. Begin with a page in Dreamweaver that contains a large image. Click the image to select it.

2. Choose the rectangular Image Map tool.

3. Click and drag over the region that you want to make "hot," as shown here.

4. With the image map selected (or the button, link, or slice if you are using these methods), open the Behaviors panel and click the plus sign.

5. Choose Open Browser Window from the list and the Open Browser Window dialog box will appear.

6. Click the Browse button and choose the page that you want to open as a pop-up window. (This is just a regular HTML page.)

7. Choose the size of the window, in pixels, by entering information in the Width and Height fields.

8. If you want to open the windows "clean"—meaning just the window will open and no menus or toolbars—uncheck all the Attributes boxes. (The attributes are self explanatory.)

9. Click OK and test your pop-up in a web browser, as shown in Figure 11-18. The window should now work, but you may notice an unusual behavior. The window opens as soon as the mouse hovers over the area without your even having to click. Let's fix this.

Figure 11–18: The pop-up window.

10. If you look in the Behaviors panel, you will see the new behavior with a little gear next to it. In the left column, you will see onMouseOver—we want to change this to a clicking action.

11. Click the arrow that opens the drop-down menu and choose onClick.

> **NOTE**
>
> These are JavaScript actions—but don't worry, because you don't have to do any coding. That's what the behaviors are for.

12. Now test in the browser and the pop-up should work correctly.

Closing a Window

We could have visitors close the windows through menus and buttons, but let's do something a bit more elegant—create close buttons.

1. In Dreamweaver, type the word **CLOSE** at the bottom of the page. You next need to attach a link so that the text becomes clickable.

2. Highlight the text, and then type a pound sign (#) into the Link field of the Property Inspector, as shown in Figure 11-19. Using the pound sign is a good way to attach code to a blank link. (Actually, the # is used for sending the browser to a named anchor. Since the anchor has no name, it will just function as a blank link.)

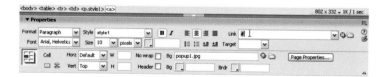

Figure 11–19: Making the text link active.

3. Switch to Code view or Split view and locate the line of code that contains the CLOSE text. If you highlight the text, it will appear highlighted in code view.

4. Click the mouse after the # code and before the > tag. Enter the following code:

```
onClick="window.close()"
```

It should look like this:

```
<p align="center" class="style1"><a href="#" onClick="window.close()">CLOSE</a></p></td>
```

That's all the code you need to create. If you test the window now and click the Close link, the window will close.

Creating a Close Button

Adding a button is similar to what you have just done with the text, except it's all done with one line of code.

Insert this code before the closing </body> tag. Enter the following code exactly as shown here:

```
<input type="button" name="Button" value="close" onClick="window.close()">
```

- The first part, `<input type="button" name="Button"`, tells the browser to create a button named *button*.

- The next part, `value="close"`, just adds the word *close* as a label; you could name it anything you wanted, such as "make this window go away."

- The `onClick` part tells the browser that something will happen when the button is clicked with the mouse.

- `"window.close()"` is what will happen after the click. The window is addressed first and then it is told to close. The statement is then closed with a > tag.

Figure 11-20 shows an example of the button added to a pop-up window.

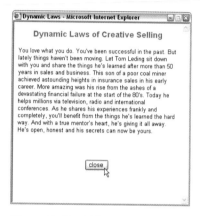

Figure 11–20: Adding a Close button to a page.

JUMP MENUS

Jump menus are those nifty little drop-down menus that allow you to select an option that "jumps" to a new web page. These are useful for adding navigation where space is limited. They also offer a clean and intuitive navigation system.

> **NOTE**
>
> Don't confuse jump menus with drop-down menus. They are not the same.

1. In Dreamweaver, click where you want the menu located.

2. Choose the Forms option from the Insert bar.

3. Click the Insert Jump menu button:

4. The Insert Jump Menu dialog box will open. Type the text that you want the viewers to see into the Text field.

5. Click the Browse button and locate the page to which you want the viewer to go in the URL field. Alternatively, you can enter the URL directly. Figure 11–21 shows the options entered for the first item.

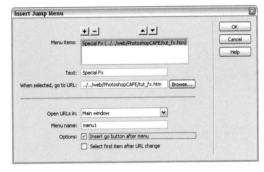

Figure 11–21: Filling out the options for the jump menu.

6. Click the Insert Go Button After Menu option to add a button labeled "Go." The user will choose an option and then click the button to go to the page. Otherwise, the user will choose the option and go directly to the page without doing anything else. Which option you prefer is simply a matter of taste.

7. Click the plus button to add another item.

8. Continue steps 5–7 until you have added all your desired links.

9. Click OK to add the jump menu to the page. A form field will be added automatically to make it work.

Figure 11-22 shows the jump menu in action.

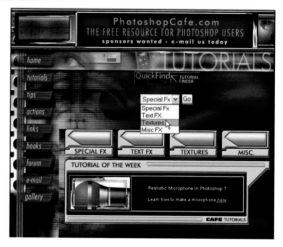

Figure 11–22: The jump menu.

BUILDING A LIQUID SITE

Have you ever wondered how to make your web site stretch to fit the browser as it's expanded? The latest term for this technique is *liquid*, because the site flows like liquid to fill the entire browser window, no matter what size the browser is.

> **NOTE**
>
> When I started designing web pages in 1994, when all this stuff was new, liquid was the only way you could design a site. All sites were liquid! Then, tables were used for laying out pages and designers chose to constrain the design to a set size to control text wrapping and image placement.

You can build liquid sites and constrain certain parts of the page while allowing other parts to reflow. That is what we are going to do here.

At the heart of liquid sites are seamless repeating backgrounds and tables that use percentages rather than pixels. This makes sense, because 760 pixels will always be 760 pixels, whereas 100 percent will be the entire width of a screen at 640x480 and also 1600x1200 pixels. People choose the liquid style to fill browsers no matter what resolution viewers have set their screens to or how large people expand or contract their browser windows.

> **TIP**
>
> Don't design all your sites as liquid, because you lose control of formatting, but in some cases it is the perfect solution.

1. Create a new page in Dreamweaver and insert a new table, like the one shown in Figure 11-23. Here, I have chosen two rows and two columns and then merged the top two columns. You can do the same or choose a different configuration.

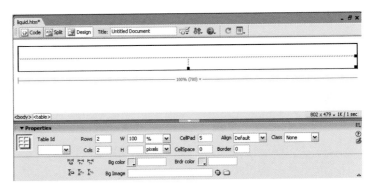

Figure 11–23: Setting the table width to 100 percent so it will stretch with the browser.

2. Select the entire table using the tag selectors in the status bar of the page.

3. Under the width field (W), enter a setting of **100** and choose % from the option on the right, as shown in Figure 11-23. Choose 0 for the Border to make it invisible.

4. Let's decorate the top bar with an image. Create a seamless repeating background in Photoshop. (Chapter 2 shows you how to do this.)

5. Select the top cell of the table. (This will be the header.)

6. Click the BG Image folder in the Property Inspector and locate the image to be used as the background, as shown in Figure 11–24.

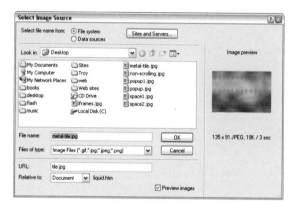

7. Click OK. The image will load and repeat to fill the cell.

Figure 11–24: Choosing the background image.

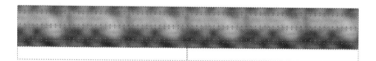

8. You need to set the page margins to 0 or an unsightly gap will appear around the entire page and the edge of the browser window. Launch the page properties by choosing Modify | Page Properties or pressing CTRL-J (CMD-J).

9. Figure 11-25 shows the Page Properties dialog box and the margin settings. Enter **0** into each field. A blank setting will cause a gap to appear.

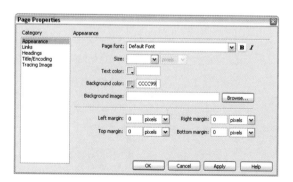

Figure 11–25: Setting the page margins to 0.

10. We have selected a background color of CCCC99. This will color the entire page but not override areas that have an image set as a background. Background images always take preference over color in the hierarchy of things.

11. Click OK to apply the settings.

12. Insert the images and/or text that you want to put in the left column. Let's make this column a fixed size that will change with the rest of the page.

13. Click and drag on the cell divider to size the left column, as shown in Figure 11–26.

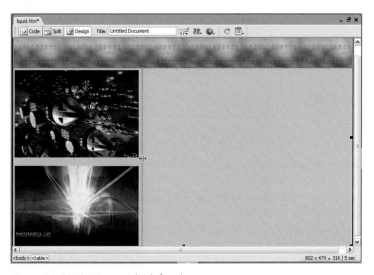

Figure 11–26: Setting up the left column.

14. Select the left cell (or any cell to which you want to apply a fixed width). In the width field (W) of the Property Inspector, change the numerical setting to a size in pixels (in this case, 300).

15. Add the content (text and/or images) to the right column. Keep the width field blank in the Property Inspector. The column with a size specified in the width field will always be the specified width. The rest of the cells will expand or contract to fill the browser window.

16. Test the page by launching it in the web browser and making it narrow, as in shown Figure 11-27. Notice how everything fits well and the header is repeating.

Figure 11–27: Testing at a narrow width.

17. Expand the browser window, as shown in Figure 11-28, and notice that the page has expanded to fit the window. The text will automatically rewrap to fill the space. Also notice that the width of the left column is still the same. This is a liquid page in action.

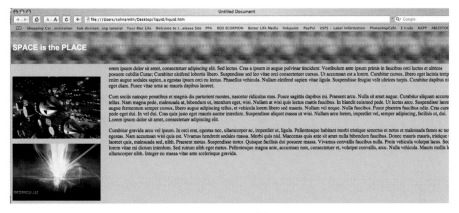

Figure 11–28: The expanded window and the site still fits.

TIP

To prevent the liquid column from collapsing beyond a certain width, try this crafty little trick: Create an image in Photoshop that's 1 pixel high, and make the width the size of your minimum desired width for the column. Hide the background layer and save the image as a transparent GIF. Insert it as an image in the bottom of your table cell, and the column will not be able to contract smaller than the image.

CHAPTER 12

GOING LIVE: UPLOADING YOUR SITE TO THE WEB

You have created your new web site and now it's time to show it off to the rest of the world. Presently, your fabulous labor of love is sitting on your local computer, going nowhere. In this chapter, we'll walk through everything you need to do to get your precious work on the Net. We will sign up for a hosting account, register a domain name, configure Dreamweaver, and finally upload it all to the Web. After that, we will wrap things up with a few housekeeping tips you can use to maintain your sites with power and ease.

OBTAINING A HOSTING ACCOUNT

Before the world can see your site, you need to put it onto a computer that is permanently connected to the Internet. This is called a *web host*. You can get a hosting account with a service provider. Many companies provide this service at various prices; some are even free, but they usually have some drawbacks. Free accounts tend to be pretty slow and some have limited features and support options. In addition, many free accounts are blocked for libraries and schools in an effort to cut down on the availability of online porn and other sites not suitable for young eyes. The plus is, of course, they are free.

As far as paid hosting goes, you can pay all kinds of prices, from a few dollars a month to several hundred, depending on features and bandwidth (the amount of traffic your site receives). Some good hosts in the United States are **http://www.mediatemple.net**, **http://www.lunarpages.com**, and **http://www.namesarecheap.com**. These service providers offer good solutions at reasonable prices. Check out the book site at **www.dreamweavercafe.com/book** for links to some web hosts.

For the sake of illustration, let's walk through the process using mediatemple.net; whatever host you decide to use, the sign-up process will probably be similar, and most companies offer good step-by-step instructions online.

1. Log onto the page of your chosen host. In this case, it's **www.mediatemple.net**.

2. Click the Get Started link (at the

top of the page) and choose Order Services from the menu that appears.

Some hosts will give you the option to register a domain name (your-name.com) at this time. Some will offer a really good deal, and others will offer a free name with the hosting account. (We will look at registering a name separately in the next tutorial.)

3. In this case, I entered my existing domain name: **dreamweaver-cafe.com.** Click Next.

4. Choose the Shared Server option, as shown. Your web site will share a computer with other web sites—this is the most economical option.

5. All the different types of accounts available are then presented. I chose the most economical account for $9.95 per month. (Prices will vary from time to time and from host to host.) Keep in mind that you can always upgrade your account if the need arises.

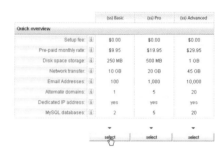

6. Choose your payment options. Most hosts will offer a discount if you pay a year or so up front. (Note that if you are not satisfied with the service, you can always demand a refund later.) In this case, you have to pay two years in advance to get the best rate of $9.95 per month.

7. Click Next.

8. Enter the information about the owner of the site—you or your client.

9. Click Save.

10. Finally, enter your credit card information to pay for the account. Look for the locked padlock icon in the corner of your web browser to indicate that this page is secure. If you are uncomfortable with the security of the online pay process, find the host's tele-

phone number on the web site
and sign up over the phone.

The next thing to do is to check your e-mail. You should receive a
confirmation letter with instructions for uploading your site and connecting your e-mail. Most hosts will provide a "control panel" that
you can log into, where you set up your e-mail and other tasks. When
you receive the confirmation, look for the IP address of the account,
the username, and password. You will need these to upload your site.
Here are some fictitious examples to give you an example of something to look for:

• IP address (Internet Protocol): 64.301.122.279

• FTP User Name: dwcafe

• FTP Password: YU665eTg

REGISTERING A DOMAIN NAME

If you wanted, you could keep 64.301.122.279 as your site address and it would
work fine, but most of us find it difficult to remember such strings of numbers, and

this will inhibit visitors from easily finding your web site. A better solution is to obtain a domain name, which can be anything of your choosing (providing it isn't already taken) and can end with various extensions, such as *.com*, *.net*, and *.biz*. For example, *dreamweaverCafe.com* is a domain name. Because domain names are not case sensitive, typing in *DreamweaverCafe.com*, *DreamweaverCAFE.com*, or *dreamweavercafe.com* will all get you to the same web site.

Perhaps you already have a domain name or you registered one when you signed up for the hosting account. If you already have a name, I will show you what to do with it in the upcoming "Linking Your Domain Name with Your Hosting Account" section. Otherwise, here's how to get one:

1. Find a name provider of your choosing. For the sake of this exercise, use **http://www.networksolutions.com**. This is the best known and oldest of the name providers. (By the way, Network Solutions used to be called Internic and was the only company that issued domain names until the Domain Name Industry in the United States was deregulated a few years ago.)

2. Enter your desired name (**mydesiredname**, in this case) and choose the extensions you are interested in. I chose .com because it is still the most popular extension used in the United States.

3. Click Search.

4. After a reasonable amount of time, the page will return the results of your search, like the page shown in Figure 12-1, to let

you know whether your name is available or already taken. We are in luck—mydesiredname.com is available! It's becoming increasingly difficult to find a good name as many are already in use. To combat this, more extensions are being introduced, such as .biz. If your domain name is already taken, try a different extension or a different name altogether until you find one you like that is available.

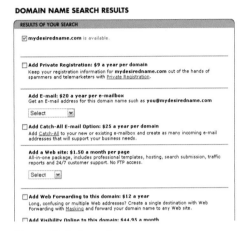

Figure 12–1: A results page.

TIP

If you want to find out who currently owns a domain name, click the Whois Lookup search option on the domain name provider's site.

5. Follow the prompts to pay for the name and make it yours. You will pay an annual fee for the name. Figure 12-2 shows the billing page on another name provider (**www.namesarecheap.com**) for a bit of variety and cheaper options.

Figure 12–2: Buying the domain name.

EXTRA FEATURES

Look for a name provider who provides extra features that come with a domain name for no extra cost:

- **Parking:** The name will need somewhere to point to when you register it. A parked name will point to an "Under construction" page.

- **Domain Forwarding:** When visitors type in the domain name, you can choose to forward to any page you like, even sublinks. For example, when a user types in *mydesiredname.com*, he or she could be forwarded to **www.photo-shopcafe.com** or **www.photoshopcafe.com/names/books/here.htm**. This is a great way to save money by hosting several web sites on a single account.

- **URL Cloaking:** This works with forwarding but will keep the domain name in the menu bar and "cloak" the actual address of the web page. This gives the illusion of a separate hosting account.

- **E-mail Forwarding:** Same as domain forwarding, but you can choose an e-mail address that will catch all the e-mail that is sent to that domain—an example is **webmaster@mydesiredname.com**.

LINKING YOUR DOMAIN NAME WITH YOUR HOSTING ACCOUNT

Let's say that you have now signed up for a hosting account and a domain name from different providers. (If they are both at the same place, you can skip this section.)

You will need to collect some information from your web host. Most of this information should be in your confirmation e-mail. Look for information about name servers—the server on the web host that handles the domain names and assigns them to the IP address. Usually, a primary and secondary name server will appear. Here are the addresses for Media Temple (I changed the Netaddress for security reasons):

- Primary Server Hostname: ns1.mediatemple.net

- Primary Netaddress: 219.132.221.4

- Secondary Server Hostname: ns2.mediatemple.net

- Secondary Netaddress: 219.232.220.4

Now check the confirmation e-mail that came from the name provider. You are looking for instructions on setting up your name servers. You may have a domain control panel that you will log into (otherwise, you'll find a form that you can use to send them the name server and Netaddress information that you want the domain name "pointing" at).

1. Log into the domain panel using the provided link, username, and password. (Usually, the username is the domain name.)

2. Click Manage Domain Names or Name Servers.

3. Enter the Name Servers into the provided fields. The Net address will be displayed automatically (Namesarecheap.com panel shown).

4. Once you have assigned the names, it will take from 24 to 48 hours for the names to "resolve" (that is, for them to be updated in the central database and be usable to you). While you are waiting for the names to be resolved, you can use the supplied IP address to upload your pages.

UPLOADING YOUR PAGES TO THE WEB SERVER

Now that we have sorted out the hosting and domain names, we can upload all the files to the web server. It's important that you keep the directory structure intact. If your images are in a folder called Images, they should be uploaded in a folder also called Images. If you rearrange the way the files are organized, it will break the file links and cause items to be missing from the web page. If you upload the HTML pages only, none of the images will show up. You must upload everything to the web server that you want to appear on the final site; if it's not there, the viewers will not be able to see it.

Connecting Dreamweaver to the Web Server

The good news is it's easy to upload using Dreamweaver; it can even scan your site for broken links. First, enter the correct settings so that Dreamweaver can connect to the web server.

1. Open the Site Definition window by choosing Site | Manage Sites.

2. Select your site in the window and click the Edit button.

3. Choose the Advanced tab from the top of the Site Definition window.

4. Choose Remote Info from the menu on the left.

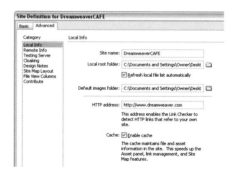

5. Under Access, choose the FTP (File Transfer Protocol) option.

6. Enter the settings that you received from your web host:

- **FTP Host:** This will be your domain name. If you don't have one yet or it's not set up yet, you can use the IP address you received from your web host.

- **Host Directory:** This is the folder on your server where your HTML pages will reside. This should also be included in your confirmation letter from your web host. The most common are html/ and public_html/. If you leave this blank, you can still log into the site, but you will be at the root and will need to navigate to the correct folder to upload the files manually.

- **Login:** This is your FTP username.

- **Password:** This is your FTP password.

  Your settings should look similar to this.

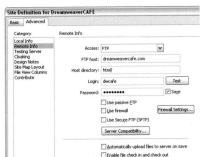

7. Click the Test button and wait for a dialog box that will say either that you have connected to the web server successfully or that an error occurred. If you receive an error message, make sure that your computer is connected to a working Internet connection, that you have entered all the fields correctly, and that you have used the correct case for the username and password. Also, make sure that no spaces were accidentally entered into any of the fields. Try substituting the IP address for your domain name. (Perhaps it isn't resolved yet—see the section on domain names earlier in the "Linking Your Domain Name with Your Hosting Account"

section.). If it still doesn't work, you will need to contact your web host to track down the problem.

8. Click the OK button in the Site Definitions window.

9. Click OK (or Done) in the Site Manager.

Uploading the Site to the Web Server

After you have successfully set up Dreamweaver on the web server, you can upload the site.

1. Choose Window | Files or press F8 to open the File Manager.

2. Expand the window so that you can see both the Local and the Remote windows.

3. Click the button to connect to the remote host, as shown here. You will also click this button to disconnect. This button will turn green when a connection has been established.

4. When you connect to the remote server (host), you will see files or folders. Not much is shown here because you have not yet uploaded the site.

5. Choose the files that you want to upload from the Local window. If you want to upload the entire site, select the main top folder.

6. Click the Put Files (upload) button, shown next, and any selected files will be uploaded to the remote server. (If you selected the topmost folder, a message will appear: "Are you sure you want to put the entire Site?" Click Yes.)

7. You will see a message saying "Include dependent files?" This means that Dreamweaver will scan for any embedded files such as images and upload those to their correct paths. If you are uploading the entire site, it is not necessary to include dependent files because they are already being uploaded. If you are uploading a new page that has a few images, clicking Yes will save you having to locate the images and upload them separately.

TIP

You can also upload (put) and download (get) files by clicking and dragging them from one window to the next. Wherever you drag them to is where they will go. If you need to store the file in a folder, drag it to the folder.

You will now see some activity in the files window as the files are being uploaded to the web server. When Dreamweaver has finished, the files will appear in the Remote window, as shown in Figure 12-3. Congratulations! Pop open a bottle of bubbly; your site is now live on the Internet and can be viewed from a web browser!

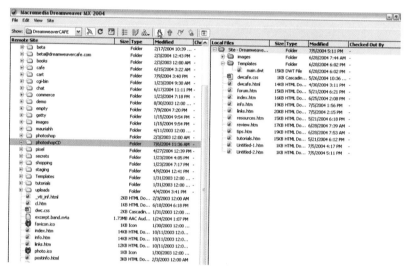

Figure 12–3: The uploaded site.

MAINTAINING AND MANAGING YOUR SITE

Now that the site has been uploaded to the Internet, you can't just let it sit stagnant like a printed brochure. A web site is *organic* and needs to be updated with fresh content from time to time. Let's look at some tools to help you manage your site.

Synchronization

Here is a scenario. You have been updating the site from several different computers, or someone else has been updating it. You are not quite sure if all the latest files are on the remote or local server. Perhaps you have made changes to several pages and have forgotten which pages have been changed.

The solution is a feature called synchronization. This will scan all the files on your computer and on the remote host, compare the two, and alert you to the differences. You can then choose to download all the missing files or newer versions to your local computer or to upload to the web server.

1. Open the File Manager in Dreamweaver.

2. Choose your site from the Sites window.

3. Connect to the site by clicking the Connect button.

4. Right-click the top-level folder in either the Remote or Local view and choose the Synchronize option.

5. Click Synchronize Now.

6. You will see the Synchronize Files dialog box with several options:

   - **Synchronize:** Synchronize the entire site or a selected folder.

   - **Direction:** Place the newest files on the remote server or your local desktop.

   - **Delete remote files not on local drive:** Remove any files that are no longer used on the remote server. Be very careful using this option so that you don't delete any files you need.

7. Click the Preview button.

8. Dreamweaver will conduct a scan and then open a box like the one shown next. No files have been changed yet.

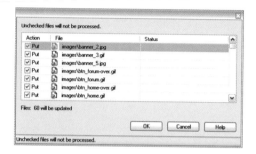

9. All the selected files will be changed. If you do not wish to include a file, unselect it by clicking the box to the left of its name.

10. Click OK to perform the process.

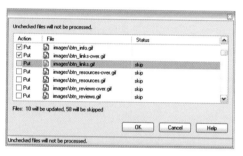

11. Figure 12-4 shows the window after the synchronization is complete. It will display how many files have been updated and how many have been skipped (those you unselected).

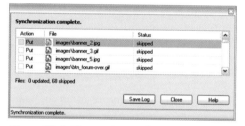

Figure 12–4: The results window.

Checking for Broken Links

It's frustrating for visitors to click a link, only to receive an error message. This message means that something is wrong with the link or that the page no longer exists. If this happens too many times on your site, visitors will go elsewhere. You can use Dreamweaver to check for any broken links.

1. Open the File Manager window.

2. Choose Site | Check Links Sitewide or press CTRL-F8 (CMD-F8).

3. Click the green arrow at the top left and choose Check Links For Entire Site.

You can also choose the Check Links For Selected Files/Folders In Site option to check a single page or a folder.

You can check three types of results from the Show drop-down menu: Broken Links, External Links, or Orphaned Files.

BROKEN LINKS

All the links that are going to pages or images that are problematic will be displayed, as shown in Figure 12-5. You will need to go in and manually repair each link. Make sure that the names of the links are entered correctly and the files are present.

Figure 12–5: Broken links.

> **TIP**
>
> Run synchronization first—this will fix some of the problems for you.

EXTERNAL LINKS

Figure 12-6 shows some *external links*, links to other web sites, e-mail, and services outside of your own web page. Exchanging links with other similar sites is a great way to increase your traffic and your ranking with search engines such as Google.

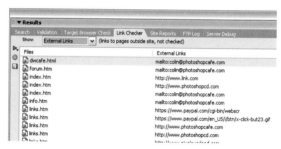

Figure 12–6: External links.

ORPHANED FILES

Orphaned files, like those shown in Figure 12-7, are files with no links attached. Usually, these files can be safely removed from the web server. (Check them each first, though, to be sure they are no longer needed.)

Figure 12–7: Orphaned files.

CONCLUSION

Congratulations! If you have worked your way through this book, you are now able to build and upload web sites the same way the pros do it. The next step is to keep experimenting, try building more sites and trying new things, and wander from the examples in the book and create something entirely different using the skills you have gained. Check out the book site at **www.dreamweavercafe.com/books** for more tips and updates. Happy web site building!

INDEX

SYMBOLS

_ (underscore), 221
- (dash), 221
/ (slash), 111, 272

A

Accessibility options, 234
aligning, 48–50
    content boxes, 153–154
alpha channels, 103
alt text, 91
anchors, 179
animated GIFs, 209
animation
    adding to your web page, 217–218
    fading, 215–216
    key animation frames, 211
    looping, 216
    making boxes appear, 213–214
    sliding, 209–218
    tween, 211–212
anti-spam legislation, 240
aqua gel buttons, 44–46
artifacts, 101
auto slices, 67, 69
    converting to a user slice, 68

B

backgrounds
    repeating, 146–149
    seamless, 29–32
    textures, 25–26
    tiling, 26–29
    See also color; liquid sites

banding, 99
behaviors, 223
    creating rollovers using, 224–225
    removing, 225
brightness, 14
    See also color
broken links, 187, 306–307
browsers. See web browsers
brushes, 26
buttons
    adding hyperlinks to, 90–91
    adding to the main page, 47–48
    aqua gel, 44–46
    Buy Now button, 248–256
    close button, 281–282
    glassy, 42–43
    linking, 49
    navigation, 40–42
    Reset button, 238–239
    Submit button, 238
    tabbed, 47
Buy Now button, 248–256

C

cable modems, 94–95
Cascading Style Sheets. See CSS
cells, 65
centering tables, 145
checkboxes, 239–240
cloaking, 298
Clone Stamp tool, 30–31
close button, 281–282
Collapse button, 127–128
color
    analogous colors, 23–24
    brightness, 14
    changing a color's name, 22
    choosing colors, 15
    color wheel, 23
    colorizing tables, 138
    combinations, 22
    complementary colors, 24–25
    cool colors, 15
    hexadecimal colors, 18–19
    hue, 14
    hyperlink states, 180
    indexed color mode, 100
    libraries, 20–21
    PANTONE, 21
    saturation, 14
    selecting from an existing image, 18
    temperatures, 15
    text, 150
    warm colors, 15
    web-safe colors, 18–19, 21
    See also Color palette; Color Picker; patterns; Swatches palette
Color palette, 16
    building, 19
    restricting to web-safe colors, 18
Color Picker, 16–17
    restricting to web-safe colors, 18
compressing images, 96–97
    GIF, 97–101
    JPEG, 101–103
    PNG, 103
    SWF, 104
comps, 11–12
    creating, 37–39
connection speed, 94–95

content boxes
  aligning, 153–154
  building, 139–141
  horizontally spacing, 152
content organization, 6–7, 8
content zone, preparing, 131–134
Contribute, 174
creative discovery, 8–10
CSS, 156
  advantages of, 158
  attaching style sheets to your
    HTML page, 164
  changing the appearance of
    hyperlinks, 183–184
  creating your first CSS style,
    158–162
  CSS Style Definition dialog
    box, 184
  defining new tags in existing
    style sheets, 162–163
  embedded, 157
  external style sheets, 157
  global formatting, 157
  how it works, 157
  layers, 131
  master style sheets, 161
  modifying style sheets, 166–169
  New CSS Style dialog box, 183
  Style Definition dialog
    box, 194–195
  using style sheets, 164–165
custom content boxes
  building, 139–141
  centering tables, 145
  creating tables in
    Dreamweaver, 143
  exporting slices to
    ImageReady, 141–142
  finishing and aligning, 153–154
  formatting text, 149–151
  horizontally spacing, 152
  inserting images, 144–145
  setting an image as a repeating
    background, 146–149

D

dash (-), 221
depth, creating the illusion of, 52–55
Design view, 137
dial-up modems, 94
discovery, 6
disjointed rollovers, 89
dithering, 18, 98, 100–101
document area, 124
documents, creating new, 36–37
domain forwarding, 298
domain names, 4–5
  extra features, 298
  linking with your hosting
    account, 298–299
  registering, 295–297
downloading, 303
  calculating download time, 94–95
Dreamweaver, 3–4
  adding rollover effects, 221–222
  behaviors, 223–225
  broken chain icon, 187
  changing line spacing, 201–203
  Code view, 125–126
  Collapse button, 127–128
  connecting to the web
    server, 300–302
  creating pages from the
    File panel, 189–191
  creating rollover effects, 218–223
  creating tables, 143
  document area, 124
  drop-down menus, 226–228
  Expanded Tables mode, 129–130
  File Manager, 305–306
  Files palette, 122–123
  frames, 258–265
  importing text into, 200–201
  Insert bar, 124, 130, 232–233
  Insert Rollover Image dialog
    box, 221–222
  Manage Sites dialog box, 118, 122
  maximizing screen area, 127–128
  multitiered menus, 228–229
  opening a page, 122–123
  ordering tables, 129–130
  panels, 124
  placing images in, 198–199
  Property Inspector, 124, 128
  Reference panel, 128–129
  Select Image Source dialog
    box, 198–199
  setting the home page, 188
  setting up a new site, 118–122
  Site Definition dialog
    box, 118–122
  Split view, 126–127
  Standard Tables view, 133–134
  viewing site maps, 186–187
  workspace, 124–127
drop-down menus, 226–228
DSL, 94
duplicating elements, 48

E

e-commerce, 245
  See also PayPal
Edit in ImageReady button, 210
editable regions, 170
  defining tables as, 171–173
e-mail forwarding, 298
e-mail links, 112
Expanded Tables mode, 129–130
exporting
  pages to HTML, 113–114
  Save for Web dialog box, 115
  select slices from ImageReady,
141–142
  slices to HTML, 68–69
extensions, 4–5
external links, 308

F

fading animation, 215–216
file formats
   GIF, 97–101
   JPEG, 101–103
   PNG, 103
   SWF, 104
filenames
   Domain Names, 4–5
   extensions, 4–5
   using underscore, 221
Files palette, 122–123
Files panel, 189–191
Flash, 3
   SWF file format, 104
font, 149
   See also text
formatting text, 149–151
forms, 232–233
   allowing users to select
     multiple options, 237–238
   checkboxes, 239–240
   creating, 233–236
   creating a list/menu, 236–237
   entering parameters, 241–243
   making forms work, 241–243
   Reset button, 238–239
   Submit button, 238
frames, 209
   creating pages to load
     into, 262–263
   drawbacks to, 265
   selecting, 260
   setting properties, 261–262
   targeting frame windows,
     263–265
   using to create an image
     gallery, 258–265
   See also iframes
frameset, 258
   linking to, 265
FrontPage, 3, 4

G

galleries. *See* image galleries
Gaussian Blur, 45
GIF, 97–99
   animated, 209
   dithering, 100–101
   transparency, 206–209, 289
   See also optimizing images
glassy buttons, 42–43
global formatting, 157
Graphics Interchange Format.
   See GIF
guides, 38, 67
   creating, 70
   creating slices from, 70–71
   removing, 70
   separating zones with, 70

H

header area, 38
help, 128–129
hexadecimal colors, 18–19
hiding palettes, 266
"hit and hope" method, 9–10
home page, 111
   setting, 188
hosts
   costs, 292
   linking your domain name
     with your account, 298–299
   obtaining a hosting account,
     292–295
   settings, 301
   uploading pages to the web
     server, 300–304
HoTMetaL, 3
HTML, 2
   adding a single space, 150
   colorizing tables, 138
   exporting pages to, 113–114
   exporting slices to, 68–69
   frames, 258–265

paragraph tags, 150
   round-trip HTML editing, 3–4
hue, 14
   See also color
hyperlinks, 6–7
   active, 180
   adding, 110–112
   adding to buttons, 90–91
   anchors, 179
   broken links, 187, 306–307
   changing the appearance
     of, 179–182, 183–184
   e-mail links, 112
   external links, 308
   orphaned files, 308
   rollover, 180
   states, 180
   text, 177–179
   visited, 180
HyperText Markup Language.
   See HTML

I

iframes, 271
   creating, 272–274
   loading new pages into, 274–276
   parts of, 272
   See also frames
image galleries
   creating using frames, 258–265
   creating with Photoshop's
     automation tools, 265–270
   options, 268–270
image maps, 83–85
   attaching pop-up windows,
     277–279
   client-side, 83–84
   server-side, 83–84
ImageReady
   adding hyperlinks to buttons,
     90–91
   bundled with Photoshop, 1–2

calculating download time, 94–95
converting slices to tables, 74–75
creating rollover effects, 85–88
creating tabbed buttons, 47
Edit in ImageReady button, 210
exporting select slices from, 141–142
launching a page in ImageReady from Photoshop, 140
layer-based slices, 69, 78–79
rollover effects, 87–88
sliced sets, 81–82
targeting slices, 89
images
    animated GIFs, 209
    choosing, 32–33
    compressing, 96–97
    dithering, 18, 98, 100–101
    exporting to the web, 115
    GIF, 97–101
    inserting in tables, 144–145
    JPEG, 101–103
    mattes, 208
    measuring size and speed of, 94–95
    optimizing, 94, 95–96, 104–110, 207–208
    placing in Dreamweaver, 198–199
    PNG, 103
    proxy images, 103
    setting as a repeating background, 146–149
    SWF, 104
    transparency, 206–209
    viewing optimized images, 95–96
    watermarks, 269–270
    wrapping text around, 199
importing text into Dreamweaver, 200–201
Inconsistent Region Names dialog box, 192–193
indexed color mode, 100
index.htm, 111

inline frames. *See* iframes
Insert bar, 124
    displaying, 130
    Forms option, 232–233
Insert Jump Menu dialog box, 283
Insert Rollover Image dialog box, 221–222
inset lines, 55
interface
    creating patterns to embellish, 51
    secondary rollover, 56–59
Internet
    files on the, 4–5
    history of, 2–3
Internic, 296

J

Joint Photographic Experts Group. *See* JPEG
JPEG, 101–103
    File Size slider, 269
    See also optimizing images
jump menus, 243–245, 282–284

K

key animation frames, 211
keyframes, 211
kilobytes, 94

L

labels, 50
launching pages in ImageReady from Photoshop, 140
Layer Style dialog box, 46, 53–54
layer-based slices, 69, 78–79
Layers palette, 40, 42, 43
    rollover effects, 86–88
layouts, creating, 37–39
libraries, loading, 20–21
line spacing, 201–203
links. *See* hyperlinks

liquid sites, building, 284–289
List/Menu button, 236–237
lists, 236–238
local sites, 5
lossless format, 103

M

Macromedia Contribute, 174
Manage Sites dialog box, 118, 122
mattes, 208
menus, 236–237
    jump, 243–245, 282–284
    multitiered, 228–229
    pop-up, 226–228
Metadata tab, 266–267
multitiered menus, 228–229

N

navigation buttons, creating, 40–42
nested slices, 77
    See also slicing
nested tables, 74, 80
    creating, 134–137
    creating in Dreamweaver, 143
    See also tables
Network Solutions, 296
New dialog box, 27, 37, 40–41

O

Offset filter dialog box, 30, 31
opening pages, 122–123
optimizing images, 94
    sliced images, 104–110
    for transparency, 207–208
    viewing optimized images, 95–96
orphaned files, 308

P

Page Properties dialog box, 28, 180, 286–287
pages. *See* web pages
palettes, hiding, 266
panels, 124
    detaching and resizing, 128
PANTONE, 21
parking, 298
patterns
    creating, 51
    See also color
PayPal, 245
    creating a Buy Now button, 248–256
    fees, 256
    signing up for an account, 246–248
Photoshop
    bundled with ImageReady, 1–2
    creating image galleries, 265–270
    preparing rollover graphics in, 219–221
PhotoshopCAFE.com, 3
    launching a page in ImageReady from Photoshop, 140
PNG, 103
    transparency, 206–209
    See also optimizing images
Polygon Lasso tool, 52, 53
pop-up menus, 226–228
pop-up windows, 277
    attaching to an image map, 277–279
    closing, 280–281
    creating a close button, 281–282
Portable Network Graphics. *See* PNG
previewing, 110
Property Inspector, 124, 128
proxy images, 103

R

Reference panel, 128–129
remote connections, 5
remote rollovers, 89–90
Reset button, 238–239
resolution, screen, 36–37
rollover effects
    adding to Dreamweaver, 221–222
    creating in Dreamweaver, 218–223
    creating in ImageReady, 85–88
    creating using behaviors, 224–225
    Insert Rollover Image dialog box, 221–222
    preparing graphics in Photoshop, 219–221
    remote rollovers, 89–90
    secondary, 56–59
    states, 85–86
    types of, 223
round-trip HTML editing, 3–4

S

saturation, 14
    See also color
Save for Web dialog box, 115, 219–220
screen resolution, 36–37
scrolling, 9
seamless backgrounds, 29–32
    See also liquid sites
Select Image Source dialog box, 198–199
Site Definition dialog box, 118–122
site maps
    applying templates to existing pages, 191–196
    basic, 7, 8
    creating pages from the File panel, 189–191
    renaming existing pages, 196
    setting the home page, 188

updating, 197
    viewing in Dreamweaver, 186–187
sites. *See* web sites
slash (/), 111, 272
Slice Select tool, 68, 78
Slice tool, 62, 64, 78
slicing, 63–65
    adjusting adjacent slices, 75
    auto slices, 67, 68, 69
    avoiding stray slices, 77
    combining slices, 71–73
    converting multiple slices into a table, 79–80
    converting slices to tables, 74–75
    creating slices, 66–67
    creating slices from guides, 70–71
    exporting select slices from ImageReady, 141–142
    exporting slices to HTML, 68–69
    icons, 69
    layer-based slices, 69, 78–79
    manual slicing, 76–78
    nested slices, 77
    optimizing sliced images, 104–110
    renaming slices, 83
    rollover attached slices, 69
    rollover modified state, 69
    selecting and modifying, 68
    sliced sets, 81–82
    strategies, 65–66
    targeting slices, 89
    user slices, 68, 69
    using tables to organize slices, 73–74
sliding animation, 209–213
spam, 240
Standard Tables view, 133–134
storyboards, 10
sub-links, 7
    See also links

Submit button, 238
Swatches palette, 20
   adding custom colors to, 21–22
   changing a color's name, 22
   loading swatch libraries, 20–21
   restoring factory settings, 21
SWF, 104
   See also optimizing images
synchronization, 304–306, 307

T

tabbed buttons, 47
tables, 64–65
   border thickness, 135
   cell padding, 135
   cell spacing, 135
   centering, 145
   colorizing, 138
   columns, 135
   converting multiple slices into
      a table, 79–80
   converting slices to, 74–75
   creating an empty table, 131–134
   creating in Dreamweaver, 143
   defining as editable regions,
      171–173
   Expanded Tables mode, 129–130
   headers, 135
   inserting images in, 144–145
   nested, 74, 80, 134–137
   ordering in Dreamweaver,
      129–130
   organizing slices, 73–74
   rows, 135
   Table dialog box, 135–136, 234
   width, 135
targeting slices, 89
templates, 169–170
   adding content, 176
   applying to an existing page,
      191–196

changing the appearance of
      hyperlinks, 179–182
   converting pages to, 170–171
   editable, 170
   Update Template Files dialog
      box, 181
   using, 174–175
text
   alt text, 91
   formatting, 149–151
   hyperlinks, 177–179
   importing into Dreamweaver,
      200–201
   labels, 50
   line spacing, 201–203
   wrapping around images, 199
textures, 25–26
   seamless backgrounds, 29–32
   tiled backgrounds, 26–29
Texturizer, 29
3-D look
   creating, 52–55
   inset lines, 55
tiled backgrounds, 26–29
   seamless backgrounds, 29–32
   See also textures
transparency, 206
   optimizing and matting, 207–208
   preparing the image, 206–207
Trim command, 207
tween, 211–212

U

UltraDev, 4
underscore (_), 221
Update Template Files dialog
   box, 181
uploading pages, 300, 302–304
   connecting Dreamweaver to the
      web server, 300–302
URL cloaking, 298
user slices, 68, 69

V

viewing optimized images, 95–96
views
   Code view, 125–126
   Design view, 137
   Split view, 126–127
   Standard Tables view, 133–134

W

watermarks, 269–270
web browsers, 2
   previewing in, 110
Web Content palette, 73
   creating rollover states, 87–88
web design editors, history of, 3–4
web hosts
   costs, 292
   linking your domain name with
      your account, 298–299
   obtaining a hosting account,
      292–295
   settings, 301
   uploading pages to the web
      server, 300–304
web pages
   adding animation, 217–218
   applying templates to existing
      pages, 191–196
   converting to templates, 170–171
   creating from the Files panel,
      189–191
   frames, 258–265
   opening in Dreamweaver,
      122–123
   renaming existing pages, 196
Web Photo Gallery dialog box,
   267–268
   options, 268–270
web servers, defined, 4
web sites
   creating in Dreamweaver,
      118–122

liquid sites, 284–289

maintaining, 304–308

synchronization, 304–306, 307

uploading to the web server,
302–304

See also e-commerce

web-safe colors, 18–19, 21

See also color

Whois Lookup, 297

windows, pop-up, 277–282

wireframing, 5

comps, 11–12

content organization phase, 6–7, 8

creative discovery phase, 8–10

discovery phase, 6

pulling it all together, 11–12

World Wide Web Consortium
(W3C), 2

Z

zone system, 62–63

INTERNATIONAL CONTACT INFORMATION

AUSTRALIA
McGraw-Hill Book Company
Australia Pty. Ltd.
TEL +61-2-9900-1800
FAX +61-2-9878-8881
http://www.mcgraw-hill.com.au
books-it_sydney@mcgraw-hill.com

CANADA
McGraw-Hill Ryerson Ltd.
TEL +905-430-5000
FAX +905-430-5020
http://www.mcgraw-hill.ca

GREECE, MIDDLE EAST, & AFRICA
(Excluding South Africa)
McGraw-Hill Hellas
TEL +30-210-6560-990
TEL +30-210-6560-993
TEL +30-210-6560-994
FAX +30-210-6545-525

MEXICO (Also serving Latin America)
McGraw-Hill Interamericana Editores
S.A. de C.V.
TEL +525-1500-5108
FAX +525-117-1589
http://www.mcgraw-hill.com.mx
carlos_ruiz@mcgraw-hill.com

SINGAPORE (Serving Asia)
McGraw-Hill Book Company
TEL +65-6863-1580
FAX +65-6862-3354
http://www.mcgraw-hill.com.sg
mghasia@mcgraw-hill.com

SOUTH AFRICA
McGraw-Hill South Africa
TEL +27-11-622-7512
FAX +27-11-622-9045
robyn_swanepoel@mcgraw-hill.com

SPAIN
McGraw-Hill/
Interamericana de España, S.A.U.
TEL +34-91-180-3000
FAX +34-91-372-8513
http://www.mcgraw-hill.es
professional@mcgraw-hill.es

UNITED KINGDOM, NORTHERN,
EASTERN, & CENTRAL EUROPE
McGraw-Hill Education Europe
TEL +44-1-628-502500
FAX +44-1-628-770224
http://www.mcgraw-hill.co.uk
emea_queries@mcgraw-hill.com

ALL OTHER INQUIRIES Contact:
McGraw-Hill/Osborne
TEL +1-510-420-7700
FAX +1-510-420-7703
http://www.osborne.com
omg_international@mcgraw-hill.com